PRAISE FOR
Cycling, Wine, and Men:
A Midlife Tour de France

"Cycling, Wine, and Men *is a charming, delightful, and enlightening read. I fell madly in love with Nancy Brook—her words rang true, her insights and honesty felt like a good friend. A constant reminder to live your life fully, forgive yourself daily, and love yourself more. There's a line in her book, 'There's a gift in the waiting,' which perfectly describes this gem of a memoir."*

– AMY FERRIS, author of *Marrying George Clooney, Confessions from a Midlife Crisis*

"Brook's observant tale left me longing to box up my bike and head back to France. A journey isn't about the destination, but the valleys, the climbs, and the small hamlets along the way. As she demonstrates, what you learn about yourself in the process often proves to be the ultimate souvenir."

– KATHLEEN FLINN, author of *The Sharper Your Knife, the Less You Cry*

"When it comes to heartache and relationships, many women often put healing on the back seat when maybe they should be putting it on a bike seat—literally and figuratively! This book does a wonderful job of reminding women that while the journey may be more important than the destination... sometimes the destination is just what is needed to return to happiness and contentment at home."

– KIMBERLY DAWN NEUMANN, author of *The Real Reasons Men Commit* and founder of DatingDivaDaily.com

"Honest, heartfelt, and inspiring. I admire Nancy Brook's courage to overcome challenges and explore life's possibilities."

– RICK FRISHMAN, bestselling author and Morgan James publisher

"I love the lesson of the book: looking for happiness outside of ourselves never produces lasting satisfaction."

– PEGGY MCCOLL, *New York Times* bestselling author

"Cycling, Wine, and Men is sure to inspire others to follow their bliss."

– THEO PAULINE NESTOR, author of *How to Sleep Alone in a King-Size Bed*

"If you subscribe to the notion that life is about lessons, Nancy Brook's life has a few to offer. Here's the most important one: We all need people. But sometimes, the person we need most is the one we discover in ourselves."

– CRAIG LANCASTER, author of *600 Hours of Edward* and *The Summer Son*

"Nancy Brook's chronicle of cycling through France, as a means of 're-cycling' her life, goes beyond the typical 'I survived' genre. She invites the reader to join her up and down the hills, deep into the nooks and crannies of the countryside, and into the hearts of the country folk—as she braves the terrain apart from the safety of her riding companions. Nancy literally reaches out to grab life in the very best way—on her own terms. Bravo and thank you, Nancy, for a great read and a great ride!"

– BONNIE D. GRAHAM, producer/host
"Read My Lips" on BlogTalkRadio.com

"In this captivating and delightful memoir, Nancy Brook takes us on an exploration through both the rolling hills of the French countryside and her own internal journey toward self-acceptance. We grow along with her as she cycles and examines her life and relationship choices. Cycling, Wine, and Men: A Midlife Tour de France is exquisitely written and hard to put down. A real joy to read!"

– KRISTEN MOELLER, MS, author of
Waiting for Jack: Confessions of a Self-Help Junkie – How to Stop Waiting and Start Living Your Life

"At age 43, Nancy Brook takes a long, backward look at her life: It's a path pockmarked by a husband's betrayal, cavalier lovers and a long, lonely climb up the career ladder. But there's also something else. Buoyed by remarkable resilience and an innate belief in love that refuses to be snuffed out, she embarks on a mid-life adventure bicycling through France. Riding through the bucolic French countryside and over grueling mountain passes, Nancy's tour de France quickly becomes an engaging tour de life. Honest, reflective, with more than a little sauciness, Nancy's journey becomes the reader's journey to rediscovering love, levity, and a life—well lived."

– ALLYN CALTON, editor,
Magic City Magazine

"Cycling, Wine, and Men by Nancy Brook is a touching, heartfelt tome about her rough and unfortunate time leading up to a cycling tour of France. Reading about her life and a string of bad luck that leads up to her big decision to bicycle through France is filled with tension and drama and wrestles with the idea of making it all right by taking this trip. While reading, you will find yourself rooting for her and wanting to yell out, 'Yes, go to France!' And what a time it is. Ms. Brook's first book is a must read for anyone who has ever lived through life's various trials and tribulations, just to see if it turns out okay."

– MARK STEPHEN LEVY, author of *Overland*

"Riveting! I could not stop reading."

– LINDA CASSELL, executive coach, Quantum Leap Coaching & Training

"Cycling, Wine, and Men *is a Gold Medal Winner. I started reading because author Nancy Brook is a colleague. But that's where the road divides. Newly divorced and seeking the coveted new life, Brook showed me the roadway. Sharing her personal journey, she gives us a rich book with insight, poise, and warmth. A great read for women AND men alike."*

– ERIC GELB, author and copywriter, www.PublishingGold.com

Cycling, Wine, and MEN

A Midlife Tour de France

Nancy Brook

MORGAN JAMES PUBLISHING • NEW YORK

Cycling, Wine, and MEN

ISBN: 978-1-60037-827-0 (Paperback)
Library of Congress Control Number: 2010931843

Published by:
MORGAN JAMES PUBLISHING
1225 Franklin Ave Ste 32
Garden City, NY 11530-1693
Toll Free 800-485-4943
www.MorganJamesPublishing.com

Cover/Interior Design by:
Rachel Lopez
rachel@r2cdesign.com

In an effort to support local communities, raise awareness and funds, Morgan James Publishing donates one percent of all book sales for the life of each book to Habitat for Humanity. Get involved today, visit **www.HelpHabitatForHumanity.org.**

DEDICATION

For Alex

You are my one true love. Thanks for being such a treasure in my life.

Cycling, Wine, and MEN

A Midlife Tour de France

ONTENTS

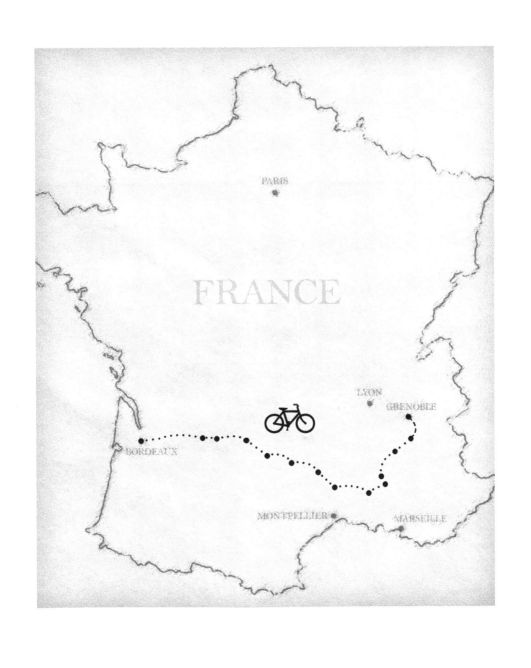

AUTHOR'S NOTE

While writing a memoir has been an experience of getting honest with myself, sharing my story with the world has required some modifications. Names and identifying characteristics of certain individuals have been changed to protect privacy. A few characters in the book are composite characters. Some time frames, details, and scenes have been adjusted for the sake of the narrative.

Bon Voyage

He said goodbye the night before I left for France with a two-word text message: BON VOYAGE. Dante's message surprised me since we hadn't talked in two weeks. I imagined him sitting alone in his downtown Billings apartment as he tapped out the letters, perched on a stool, dark head bent down with his arms resting on the small table. A summer breeze would be stirring the curtains of his open window while muffled conversations hummed from the bar patrons on the patio across the street.

Now that I'm in France, I still wonder: why did he send the message? He didn't seem to care—at least not the way I did. Our past conversations now replay in my head. When I traveled with Dante to Montreal two months ago, I was completely enthralled with him. (What woman wouldn't be with a handsome doctor who whisked her away for romance and adventure?) Then Dante told me he couldn't see a future with me and he brought up dating other women. I was hurt, then angry, and now I miss him, which I realize is plain stupid after what he said.

Still, I don't mind dwelling on Dante to distract myself from the physical agony of climbing my bicycle up this giant mountain of Provence.

It's not working. Pain shoots through my thighs with each downward thrust. My upper back and neck feel stiff from hours in this hunched-over pose. My bottom is raw from cycling more than 600 miles across France. I'm moving so slowly that horseflies are circling my head. One lands on my shoulder and digs in through my mesh jersey.

I've reached mile four. Ten excruciating miles to the top.

Keep pedaling, I tell myself.

My heart pounds, and I gasp for breath. Pro cyclists have died climbing this mountain. I might be next.

The midday sun transforms the forest into a steamy sauna. I veer from side to side, seeking patches of shade to escape the heat radiating from the asphalt. I lick salty lips and squeeze water into my mouth from a plastic bottle.

Spandex cycling clothes cling to my damp body as my pores release wine-laced sweat, remnants of my Bastille Day celebration. My God, I *am* going to die. I stop pedaling, unclip my shoes, and anchor my feet on the ground. Standing with the bike straddled between my legs, I rest my throbbing head on the handle bars.

When I booked my French vacation, I envisioned cycling, drinking wine, and practicing French. Instead, I've become a *Survivor* contestant. After nine days on the tour, I've lived through a bike wreck, a car crash, and restless nights sleeping on the ground in a leaky tent. Now I'm facing sheer hell on this soul-destroying climb up Mont Ventoux.

Did a breakup really lead me to this folly?

Chapter 1

LOOKING FOR LOVE

I t wasn't one breakup that drove me to France but all the failed relationships that had left me alone and longing for affection.

I'm now forty-three, but my search for love started when I was a teenager obsessed with romance novels. I'd swoon as I read about the handsome stranger rescuing the heroine from her struggles. I wanted a man like that—someone strong, good-looking, and passionate who could set me free.

My love life didn't turn out like the romance novels. I married at twenty-two, and a decade later, the man who had pledged eternal devotion betrayed me. We published a newspaper together in Billings, Montana, and without my knowledge he was withdrawing money out of the business checking account. I found out when a check I wrote to the printer for $2909.11 bounced.

The business had been struggling, and suddenly my only option was to shut it down and lay off my employees. I felt terrible that the check had bounced and promised the printer that I would make monthly payments of a hundred dollars, even though I had no business, no job, and no child support.

Meanwhile, my husband took off and left a mess for me. Our mortgage payments were behind, so I sold the house just before it went into foreclosure. I traded a four-bedroom home with a two-car garage for a two-bedroom apartment with off-street parking. I couldn't afford the payments on the lease for my four-year-old Honda Accord, so the car was repossessed. I rode my Schwinn ten-speed bicycle for a while until I saved $750 to buy a beat-up ten-year-old Honda with faded paint, hail damage, and a hatchback held up with a broomstick. I worked odd jobs to make money. In my spare time, I crafted a business plan to resurrect the newspaper. Money became so tight that I had to choose between food and bills. With a nine-year-old daughter to support, I chose food and skipped paying the printer.

Slowly, I shoveled my way out of the financial blizzard. One heaping shovelful led to another. I had to keep moving before I became trapped in a cold, bleak world. After eight months, the sun came out when I found two investors for the newspaper. Then, on a warm June evening, Friday the thirteenth, the dark clouds rolled in.

I heard a knock on my apartment door. I looked out the peep-hole and saw a sheriff's deputy. I had been sorting laundry and clothes covered my living room floor. My daughter, Alex, lay on the couch watching the movie *Harriet the Spy*. I opened the door, and the deputy asked me to confirm my name.

"You're under arrest for felony check fraud."

I listened in disbelief as he explained the charges. I heard the words "printer," "$10,000 bond," "jail."

"This is a mistake. My husband took money out of our account. I didn't know."

"I'm sorry," the deputy told me. "There's nothing I can do."

The deputy was kind considering the circumstances. He offered to let me call a friend to pick up my daughter so she didn't have to go into protective custody. He also didn't handcuff me in front of my neighbors. But he had a job to do, and he drove me to the county jail.

A strange series of events had landed me there. When I missed my monthly payment to the printer several months before, the printer had tried calling my business phone, but the line had been disconnected. I couldn't afford that monthly bill either. The printer, who was based in a small Montana town, must have thought I had run off, and so he visited the local sheriff's office looking for options. From there, everything escalated.

There probably hadn't been much going on that summer in that small town (think Mayberry from *The Andy Griffith Show*). Without the printer's knowledge, the sheriff's office had put out a warrant for my arrest. I didn't realize at the time that writing a bad check for an amount over $500 is a felony in Montana. The maximum penalty is ten years in the state penitentiary, a $50,000 fine, or both.

Neither my friends nor I had $10,000 to spring me, so I stayed in the county detention facility in Billings with the mostly poor and uneducated women living on the margins of society. I started out in maximum security, which I assumed all prisoners did. My cell had a metal bed with a thin foam mattress, a metal sink, and a toilet without a seat. There were more than sixty women in the double-decker cell block, most housed two per cell. My first cellmate, a young woman charged with driving without insurance, stayed with me for one night. I worried that my next cellmate might be a violent offender. Fortunately, the jail staff let me stay alone when I moved to a less secure area.

Five days later, the county sheriff's deputy drove me, handcuffed and shackled, to the "Mayberry" jail. It was surreal. I rode in the front with the deputy while three male prisoners crammed the backseat. One of the men, a counterfeiter, spoke up for me and asked the deputy to release my shackles since I wasn't a threat. The deputy apologized to me, saying he couldn't. At least I wasn't in the backseat wedged between the other inmates.

I had been a member of the Chamber of Commerce and a respected newspaper owner. And there I was, handcuffed, dressed in blue jail pajamas, and charged with a felony. *How could this be happening to me?* I remember thinking.

Unlike the barracks I left behind in Billings, this jail had around ten cells. The staff at the detention center had been all business; the small-town deputies were friendly and jocular. I appeared before the Mayberry judge after a man charged with attempted murder for brandishing a sword at a party. A friend of mine knew the judge and had called two days before to vouch for my good character. The judge released me on my own recognizance. Eventually I proved my innocence, and the charges were dismissed.

Even though I hadn't knowingly written a bad check, I wouldn't exactly call myself a victim. I hadn't realized that my husband was withdrawing money out of the business checking account because I had paid no attention to my finances. I chose to shut my eyes—to the unreconciled bank statements, the unopened credit card bills, and the husband who freely used the business debit card. And while I should have called the printer to explain my predicament, I opted to ignore him, hoping he'd go away. Jail served as my wake-up call. It was time to release the shackles that had bound me to a life of denial and face reality.

My first priority became stable employment. I found a job in marketing and began climbing the corporate ladder. After six years in the business world, I made vice president of credit cards at a bank—ironic, given my past financial troubles. Those aren't the kind of things you discuss at job interviews or share over dinner with friends. I was too ashamed to tell my story to anyone other than my closest confidants.

It took me longer to pursue romance than it did to right my finances. I waited three years after my brush with the law before I finally agreed to a blind date arranged by a friend. The man treated me nicely, and we started seeing one another. I can see now that I was desperate to be loved and at the same time afraid to open myself up. I stayed aloof until he rejected me. Then I clung on like Saran wrap, which is surprising because he really wasn't anything special. At the time, I thought he was the only man for me, just like in the romance novels. And I suffered bitterly when we broke up. So did my then-twelve-year-old daughter, who had become quite attached to my boyfriend.

After that I dated a new man every year or so, careful not to let Alex—or myself—become too emotionally involved with any of them. They all seemed perfect for me at the time: the railroader, the business owner, the lawyer. I was sequentially dumped by each of them—on the phone, in a car, in a snowstorm.

My string of revolving relationships peppered with Internet dates left me weary. Two years ago I reached a turning point when my engineer boyfriend dumped me. I didn't want to date anymore and swore off Match.com. It was September, and my daughter had just left for the university two thousand miles away. I was almost forty-two, and for the first time in my life I was living by myself. I needed an outlet, something to stave off loneliness and depression: I took up cycling.

It seemed like a good idea at the time. Within the past month, I had bought a new road bicycle on impulse. The Indian summer meant pleasant riding conditions. And physical activity had always been a good outlet for me during emotionally trying times. I began to tootle my bike through my neighborhood until the snow fell. Then I heard about a winter wind-training class, where bikes are clamped into special trainers for pedaling indoors.

I met Jeff there. I didn't know it at the time, but my friend, Charles, had encouraged Jeff to come to class to meet me. I swear I wasn't even interested in dating, yet how could I resist his soulful eyes, toned body, and dark hair with a natural curl? I'll be honest: attractive, athletic, and available men in their forties don't line the streets of my hometown of Billings. When he asked me out for a Saint Patrick's Day bike ride, I said yes.

Through the spring and early summer, everything seemed perfect. We rode our bikes together, took long walks with our dogs, and shared barbecues. Then my cursed dating pattern recurred, and we broke up. We reunited and then broke up again. By November, we had embarked on a third round of dating when his kiss delivered the knockout blow.

We had just finished walking our dogs along the banks of the Yellowstone. I loaded my hairy herding duo, Zimmer and Lucky, into the back of my SUV while his decaffeinated dog, appropriately named Sanka, jumped into his truck. After our walk, Jeff hugged me goodbye and gave me a chaste peck on the cheek.

"Why don't you want to kiss me anymore?"

He kissed me again, more passionately this time. Two days later, he called to tell me we were through.

"You're a wonderful person," he paused. "But the thing is ... you bug me."

"I bug you?" I walked from my bedroom down the hall to my kitchen.

"Yeah, you bug me. I don't know what it is, but I just can't see myself being with you"How do I bug you? There must be reasons. You just aren't telling me." My voice had a bit of an edge now. I stopped pacing and stood by the kitchen counter, my left hand grabbing the Formica to steady myself.

"I don't know what they are," he said.

"What do you mean?" My voice increased its intensity and my fingers turned white as I squeezed the counter edge.

He lowered his tone. "Nancy, I don't know what to say."

"We were happy. We had plans. We talked about a future. What happened?"

"I told you. There are just some things that bug me."

"Like what?" There had to be a way to make this work. I walked back to my bedroom and slumped down on my bed.

"I don't want to go over this again."

I didn't know what to say. I inhaled deeply and counted my breaths so I wouldn't cry. After five deep breaths, he spoke.

"It's getting late. I need to go."

After I hung up, I didn't want to be alone, so I called Kathleen, my former sister-in-law. I often joked that I maintained custody of my daughter *and* Kathleen after my divorce. She was more than a relative—she was one of my best friends. Part hippy chick, part Dear Abby, Kathleen listened to my problems with ease and grace. I don't know how she could dispense such good advice considering the challenges in her own life. She was chronically underemployed, hadn't dated in years, and always had something breaking down—her car, her refrigerator, or maybe her furnace. But no matter what the situation, she always had time to listen to my dating woes, and now I told her the details about my breakup with Jeff.

"Cry for a week," she advised.

I started right away. I put down the phone, rolled over to clutch my pillow, and sobbed myself to sleep.

After a restless night, Zimmer's nose nuzzled me awake at five. *Get up! Let's walk.* Though tired, as I stretched my arms to wake myself, I realized that I felt better—a lot better. The heartache from the night before had passed like a storm cloud moving east toward the wide-open Montana prairie.

I got up and dressed for a cold winter morning, bundling up in my ratty down jacket, fleece hat, and padded gloves. I leashed my dogs, put on my headlamp, and descended into the dark.

My thoughts turned to Jeff. This breakup marked the seventh bankrupt relationship in seven years. I was weary of my dating merry-go-round, going in circles and getting nowhere and finally falling off my plastic pony. If I wasn't cycling through men all the time, that would leave room in my life for something else. The thought of "something else" shook loose a string of questions.

If I don't have a future with Jeff—or anyone—what do I want to do with my life?

I need to shake things up—but how?

Should I move?

Change my career?

What do I want anyway?

I had no answers. Then another question formed, seemingly from outside of me.

What would make you happy, Nancy?

I smiled as I realized my answer: I want to go to France.

Chapter 2

MY FRENCH FASCINATION

Ah, France. My bicycle gliding through lush landscapes, I'd stop at charming hamlets along the way where smiling villagers wearing berets would welcome me. "Join us," they'd say. We'd sit and drink wine at a roadside café, talking for hours in French. Finally, I'd tear myself away, explaining that I must continue down the road. The vision became so vivid that within a week I applied for my passport and searched for a bike tour.

I googled "Cycling Tour France" and found many options. Some Web sites showed photos of unathletic riders on fat-tired bikes with baskets. Not challenging enough. Other sites had images of lean, ultra-fit riders climbing mountains. Too challenging.

Then I found a site called Wide Open Road Cycling Tours that seemed just right. Cyclists would travel from Bordeaux to the Alps, riding on quiet back roads during the day and camping at night. I liked camping. The photos showed people on road bikes, looking somewhat fit. Other photos showed tour members smiling for the camera while eating gourmet dinners and drinking wine. I liked good food and wine. The tour lasted fifteen days, and riders were expected to ride sixty miles a day comfortably. I could do that already. And while there were two major mountains to ascend, I figured within eight months, I could whip myself into climbing shape. The tour tempted me. But I just couldn't convince myself to sign up, despite my urge to go to France.

My fascination with France began long ago with my French uncle, Clarence. As a teenager, I'd travel to Duluth, Minnesota, to visit Aunt Evelyn and Uncle Clarence during my summer vacations. I remember the discreet half-shots of whiskey my uncle gave me more than I remember him talking about his family's home country. But I loved Uncle Clarence for his warmth and charisma, and by osmosis, I must have started loving France.

French was not taught in my small Montana high school, but as a college freshman I began studying the language. Every day on my way to French class, I'd walk past a poster of the Notre Dame de Paris cathedral. Many times, pausing by the poster, I'd imagine myself in Paris visiting Notre Dame, the Louvre, and the Eiffel Tower.

For my work-study job, I had a key to the language building. One night, I snuck into the building and peeled the poster off the wall. Remorse struck the next day when I saw the unfaded spot where the poster had once hung, but the shame of my theft vanished that night. I hung the poster near my bed so I could view the Gothic cathedral each night before I drifted off to sleep. The gargoyles on the building had kept silent vigil over Paris for centuries, and now they would watch over me.

The poster became crumpled and tattered through the years, and eventually I threw it out. But the dream remained. When I turned forty, my thoughts returned to France. Despite four years of college French, I had never mastered the language. I decided to buy myself French tutorial CDs as a birthday gift. My bathroom became the perfect language sanctuary. I'd sit in my bubble bath with a glass of red wine and repeat simple French sentences.

Je voudrais du vin rouge.

Vous parlez trop vite pour moi.

Où est la toilette?

My then seventeen-year-old daughter made fun of my French practice.

"Oh, my gawd! You should hear my mom in the bathtub," she would tell her friends, my friends, even our hairdresser. Alex would then mock me with her Peppy Le Pew accent. I didn't care. Practicing the language roused my dormant fascination of France.

Conversation would improve my French, but I didn't know any francophones in Montana. Then I came up with a great idea: I'd practice on Internet chat rooms and become proficient enough to chat *en français*. It didn't go as expected. Simultaneous dialogue boxes would pop up with French greetings.

"*Salut!*"

"*Bonjour!*"

"*Ça va?*"

I panicked. How do I respond to all of these people at once? I learned some quick French responses thanks to an online French-English dictionary. Soon, my basic college French skills returned and I could carry on simple conversations. As the chat sessions continued, I met lonely men from places like Tunisia, the Caribbean, and Algeria. They desperately sought an American sugar mama—a woman lonely enough to marry a strange foreign man bent on U.S. citizenship.

My French tutors became foreign suitors, wooing me with their sweet nothings. Here's an English version of a typical conversation:

Me: Hi. Good to see you again.

Him: Hi, baby! I've missed you! Can I get your cell phone number?

Me: Bye.

I did meet two real Frenchmen. One asked if I wanted to have an affair with him when I visited Paris. The other offered to show me his naked asshole via webcam. I declined both offers. I still wanted to speak French, but I realized that chat rooms weren't the place for me, so I put French practice aside.

Almost two years (and several break-ups) later I found my new obsession: cycling. I owe a lot of my progress to indoor wind-training classes taught by Coach Jay. The first night of class I had no clue what to expect. A classmate helped me clamp my bike into the wind trainer. Coach Jay, a super-fit man in his late forties and seven-time Hawaii Ironman finisher, walked by and told me my seat was too low and jacked it up three inches. I felt like I was toppling forward.

"Go to S-3 and pedal at 90," Coach Jay instructed during our warm up.

What did he mean? Afraid to ask, I sat on my bike in the front row and pedaled.

"What are you doing?" Coach Jay yelled at me. "You're not a little girl riding through the neighborhood. Faster!"

I didn't think my legs could turn any quicker, but I pedaled like a maniac so this crazy drill sergeant wouldn't embarrass me again. Looking around, I noticed my classmates didn't seem to have a problem turning their legs this rapidly. They talked to each other as they cycled; some even had smiles on their faces. Meanwhile, my legs numbed and my face contorted itself into a grimace. This was just the warm-up.

"Come on. Quick and snappy!" Coach Jay shouted over his microphone headset as he paced through the rows of students. If this was how he worked out, no wonder he looked so lean.

We sprinted, simulated climbing hills, and performed endurance drills. Then Coach Jay had us do one-legged drills. That first night, I didn't have cleated shoes and clip-in pedals, so I skipped pedaling one leg at a time.

"You'd better get the right gear by next class," Coach Jay told me sternly.

I had never experienced such a challenging workout in my life. By the time I finished the one-and-a-half-hour class, I was as wrung out as my sopping wet cotton t-shirt.

My goal became to survive Coach Jay's class for the next nine sessions. Proper gear might help. At the next week's class I sported new cleated shoes and pedals, a new bike jersey made of technical fabric, and a new Cateye computer to measure my RPMs.

Arriving early, I set up my bike near a friendly-looking classmate. I asked him about the terminology used the week before: S-3 at 90. He explained that "S" referred to the small chain ring, "3" meant third gear and "90" indicated the RPMs, or revolutions per minute.

"Don't worry. You'll catch on."

"I really don't know what I'm doing."

He didn't disagree, but then he smiled and pointed at my new pink-flowered jersey. "At least you look better."

I faked it until I started making it. I'd watch everyone else and imitate their motions. Week by week, my legs learned to move quicker and my body handled a greater workload. I progressed from feeling completely exhausted after class to only somewhat wiped out.

By spring I was riding outdoors and making dramatic improvement. By summer I had completed my first century ride—one hundred miles. I had forgotten how much joy I could experience while cycling, but the riding brought back memories.

As a child I had pedaled a purple, banana-seat bike through Montana's countryside on dusty back roads, the same roads that are now paved for suburban neighborhoods. Sometimes my friends and I would bike to the Yellowstone River where we'd skip rocks and wade in the rapid waters. During the summer between my college freshman and sophomore years, I would ride my brother's hand-me-down Peugeot ten-speed to work and back, thirty miles round trip each day. I traveled on the interstate without a water bottle or helmet, but no one wore helmets back then. This was the early 1980s, before seat belts and car seats were even mandatory.

As a young mother, I had added a baby seat to the back of my Schwinn and had traversed the country roads in Minnesota, where I had been living at the time. Alex, who had not even turned one, would tip her head sideways to let the wind blow on her face.

By rediscovering my love for cycling, I integrated long-forgotten pieces of myself. The little girl on the banana seat had loved to explore and venture into the world. Why had I spent years denying her a bike ride on the back roads or the France trip of her dreams? By gathering these discarded fragments, I blossomed into the real me instead of the person I thought I should be. I was cycling into a whole new life.

Chapter 3

WHY I SHOULDN'T GO TO FRANCE

Even though I really wanted to go to France, I put up obstacles for more than a month. My head and my heart had been battling and so far my head was winning the fight. Logically, the trip didn't make a lot of sense. The mind chatter relentlessly pursued me, trying to convince me to surrender my dream.

Are you crazy? You can't spend so much money on a biking trip. Drive to Washington, bring your bike, and visit wineries there.

The dollar is so weak compared to the euro. Why not wait until it rises?

Can Alex really take care of the house for three weeks? Will she walk the dogs? And if she has an emergency, how will she reach you?

What about work? Can the staff really handle it on their own?

My head had a point: there was no rational reason why I needed to go to France, ride my bike, and drink wine. My heart just wanted to go. I needed a referee to break up the fight, and so I phoned ex-sister-in-law Kathleen. She wasn't swayed by my mind's logic.

"Having a dream is a good enough reason to go. Why don't you care enough about yourself to do this for you?"

"It's so much money. I just can't." I felt my throat tighten as I said the words. The tour cost £950, which was almost $2,000 in US money. I'd also have to pay for transportation, food, and a few nights of lodging. The total bill would be between $4,000 and $5,000.

"Nancy, you're not broke and struggling anymore," Kathleen said in her best faux-counselor voice.

"I know. I just don't want to end up there again." Not with the bills piling, debt collectors calling, and the sheriff's deputy carting me off to jail.

"Things are different now. It's OK to do this for yourself." Easy for her to say. She had never been to jail, as far as I knew. I took a deep breath and let it out.

"I'm afraid. I don't want to be, but I am."

"That's understandable. But you don't have to stay stuck."

"OK. How do I get unstuck then?"

"Well, you could hire a therapist. Get to the root of your problem. Pay $95 an hour." She sounded so cheerful with the idea.

"That sounds great," I said sarcastically.

"I thought you'd say that." She laughed her big laugh on the other end of the phone line. "Or option two…"

"Which is?"

"Face yourself. Say, yes, I know there is no logical reason to go to France. But I've waited too long to live this dream."

"I *have* waited a long time," I said. "It's been twenty-five years."

"Exactly my point."

"So you really think I should book the trip?"

"Yes!" she shouted. She had become my pied piper of irrational decision-making. Despite my misgivings, I could see she had a point.

"OK. I'll think it over. Thanks, Kath. I'm glad I kept custody of you in the divorce."

"You are *soooo* lucky," she said, and we laughed together.

She was right: a dream was a good enough reason to go. As a single woman on my own, it was up to me to make my own dreams come true. No one else would do it for me.

A few days later on Christmas Eve, I logged onto the Wide Open Road Web site, sipping red wine as I entered my credit card number for my deposit. *Merry Christmas*, I said to myself. Then I closed my eyes and clicked SUBMIT before my mind could change my heart.

PREPARING FOR A BICYCLE TOUR

- **Know your mileage.** You'll want to be able to ride the longest daily distance and the average weekly distance before the tour.

- **Begin cycling at least six months before your tour.** This is especially important if you're not an experienced cyclist.

- **Build up miles gradually.** If your tour averages fifty miles a day, that means you'll be riding 350 miles in a week. When you start, you may only be fit enough to accomplish fifty miles in a week. As your fitness level improves, add on more miles each week until you can comfortably cycle the weekly distance.

- **Ride five to six days a week.** Is time a factor? Incorporate cycling into your daily life. Ride to work or to run errands. All the mileage will add up to help build your endurance. On weekends, increase distance, eventually riding more than the longest ride on the tour.

- **Ride indoors.** For those who live in colder climates, buy an indoor trainer for your bicycle so you can ride inside even when the weather is nasty.

19

- **Learn basic bike mechanics.** Know how to change a flat, patch a tube, and clean and lubricate your chain.

- **Know how to fuel.** Many products on the market provide quick energy for cyclists such as sports drinks, gels, and bars. Use these before you travel to know which fuel works best for you. Take your favorite fueling products with you because they may not be available at your destination.

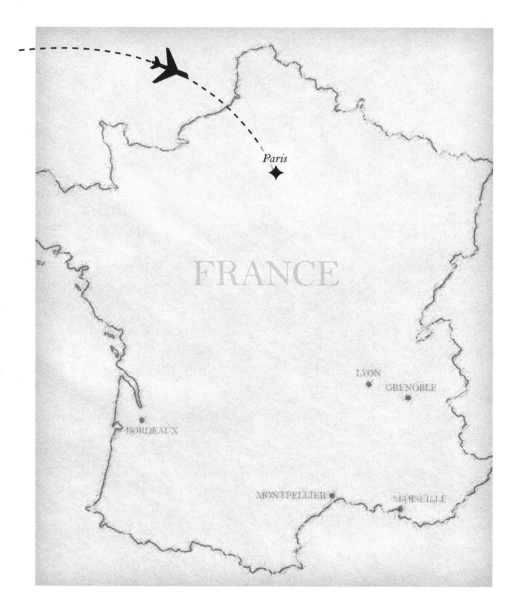

ROUTE NOTES: *Travel by plane from Billings, Montana, through Salt Lake City and on to Paris, France.*

DISTANCE: *5,547 miles or 8,927 kilometers*

Chapter 4

THE JOURNEY BEGINS

More than six months later, on the third of July, I'm leaving for France. I should be floating to the ticket counter, but I'm bogged down with an overloaded backpack and a four-by-three hard-shell bike case. The wheels of the heavy case make a rhythmic "thunk, thunk, thunk" as they roll over the tile seams inside the airport, announcing my arrival.

My daughter, Alex, follows behind as my entourage, wheeling two black suitcases. Alex is a college softball pitcher and has just finished her sophomore year. She's dressed in her baggy softball shorts with her long hair in a bun. I can tell she's unhappy as she stops by the roped line to the ticket counter and releases an exaggerated sigh.

"These suitcases are hurting my arms." Funny, since her arms are strong from pitching. I guess it's a daughter's prerogative to whine sometimes. My motherly response is to smooth things over.

"I know. We're almost there. Come on."

After I have checked in, Alex walks me to the security gate, and we hug goodbye.

"I love you, sweetie."

"I love you, too, Mommy. Don't worry about a thing! I'll be just fine. Have a fun time in France."

Don't worry? I *am* leaving a twenty-year-old home alone for three weeks. What mischief would she get into without me? Then again, she has lived on her own at college for two years. Is this *really* different?

Passing through security, I wait for the departing flight to Salt Lake City. From there I'll catch my plane to Paris. As I peer out the airport windows, I see a hazy sky caused by Canadian fires to the north and the brown landscape typical for summer in south central Montana. What scenes await me in France?

At age forty-three, this marks my first trip outside the North American continent. I've dreamt of visiting France for more than twenty-five years, but life took a different path. College, marriage, work, a baby, divorce, single parenthood, a master's degree—all came first. I made these choices, which I don't regret. Yet somehow I lost a piece of myself.

What happened to the girl who had longed to speak French, paint, and travel the globe? I had moved away from Montana to go to college with dreams of a bigger life. Deep down I had longed to be an artist but instead decided to study more practical things like business. Rather than living my life with adventure and creativity, I had settled for the stability and routine of a banking career. Maybe it's not too late to make a shift; I can still bring a piece of that girl into my life.

Even worse than living in a rut has been my tumultuous post-divorce dating. After Jeff dumped me, I really didn't intend to date again. Then, two months after I booked my French vacation, my friend Charles played cupid again and set me up with Dante. It started out so promising, and I fell for him immediately.

The first week we met, we spent every evening together. He was smart, witty, and adventurous—not to mention handsome. But there were signs along the way, signs I chose to ignore.

He was honest from the beginning, telling me that he didn't want a commitment with anyone. Dante split his time between Montana and Vermont as a locum tenens doctor, and he thought long-distance relationships were too burdensome. We could enjoy the time we had together, but he made no promises or plans for the future.

I heard his words, but I also could feel his affection and desire for me. My heart felt happy to be with him, and that is what I listened to. And as I inched closer emotionally, he responded with jabbing comments. "Doesn't it bother you that I'll be on dates with other women?" he asked me one night after dinner as we sat on my couch, my head resting on his chest.

The dagger pierced my heart. I kept my eyes closed for a few moments to push back the tears. Then I lifted my head, looked him in the eye, and calmly replied, "I'm not worried about it. I'm going to France in a few weeks, and I won't be thinking about you."

The last time I saw him, he told me once again that he couldn't see a future with me. How could he treat me so coldly?

"You're a jackass," I replied.

Dante hasn't talked to me since, aside from his text message wishing me *bon voyage* on my trip.

No point in dwelling on him anymore. I've checked in my luggage, and now I'll set down life's baggage, walking away from my responsibilities, work, and countless love mishaps. All I need is my bike and the wide open road of France.

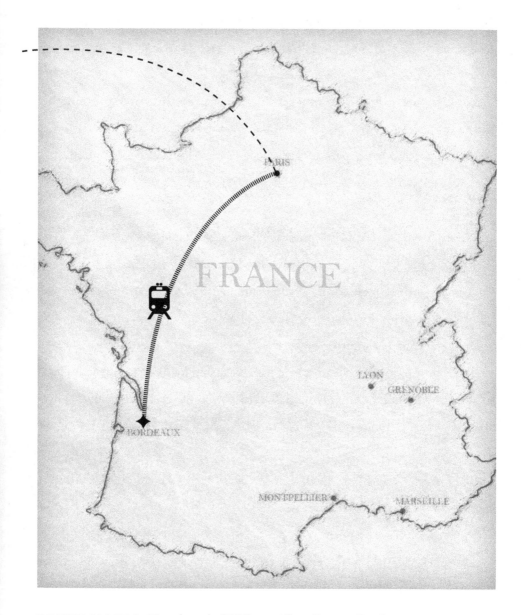

ROUTE NOTES: *Travel on the TGV train from Paris to Bordeaux.*

DISTANCE: *363 miles or 584 kilometers*

Chapter 5

INDEPENDENCE
IN FRANCE

Arriving at the Charles de Gaulle Airport, I'm rushed to find my train to Bordeaux. The depot for the TGV (*Train à Grande Vitesse* or high-speed train) is located within the airport but I don't know where to go. No signs say: "Train this way."

"Où est le train à Bordeaux?" I ask several people. When they finally figure out what I'm saying, they all answer in French, too quickly for me to understand.

For a time, I haul my bike case and two suitcases on a cart, but I leave the cart behind when I take a wrong turn down an elevator. Now I'm walking with my backpack strapped to my shoulders. I wheel the bike case in my right hand. I've stacked the small suitcase atop the large one, securing the two with a strap, jury-rigged for the purpose. These I pull in my left hand. Every twenty paces, the small suitcase lists sideways and I stop to rebalance it. I stumble on, stopping again and again to adjust my bags. Riding my bike up the Alps will be a cinch compared to this strenuous workout.

Finally, I make it to the train station with twenty minutes to spare. When the train to Bordeaux arrives, I ask the porter about my seat in car seventeen. He tells me that my car is down the tracks, about two hundred feet away. I attempt to sprint but pulling my unbalanced luggage with each hand slows me to a jog. At last I reach car seventeen and struggle to lift up my belongings.

People push by me, stepping around my load. No one will lend a hand until a middle-aged Indian woman dressed in a colorful sari sees my predicament and starts to assist me. Her efforts shame a young Indian man, maybe her son, into dropping his cigarette and helping me to lift and stow the luggage.

"Merci beaucoup," I say to him. Somehow, my thank you seems inadequate for the appreciation I feel.

I find my seat on the train by the window facing backwards. It feels good to relax at last. I'm tired from my overnight plane travel and smelly from my airport suitcase workout. Dressed in athletic clothes with my hair in a ponytail, I look the antithesis of Parisian sophistication. But I am *really* in France and on my way to Bordeaux. I can't believe I've finally made it here! It's the Fourth of July, and I am free from the suitcases at last—or at least until my train arrives in Bordeaux.

While lugging suitcases through an airport in a foreign country isn't an everyday occurrence, I'm certainly an expert at hauling a heavy load. After all, it has been just me carting the burden of single parenthood, using my wits and perseverance to make it through. Even when I've felt worn down, there has been no choice but to carry on.

I raised my daughter on my own from the time she was nine. She was an active girl who loved to play sports. After work and on weekends, I would cart her to practices around the city. The worst time of year was the spring, when she would play basketball and train for her softball season. Sometimes she'd have two practices in an evening—one on one end of town, the other half an hour in the other direction. Her dad lived two states away, so it was always up to me to be the chauffeur.

Her sessions could take up most of my evenings, but I did what I could to be efficient. I might squeeze in a workout by dressing in my running gear and jogging outside. Other times, I'd plan a shopping expedition that could be completed in the time allotted.

After practices, there was always dinner to cook. Usually, we had easy-to-prepare meals like Crock-Pot roast, soup and sandwiches, or tacos. Friday was always pizza night; we'd eat in the living room while watching a movie.

As the years wore on, my weekends became even more hectic. I'd drive to the hinterlands of Montana for basketball and softball tournaments, sometimes staying overnight. There were even a few out-of-state tournaments that we'd travel to.

Alex played three sports a year as a high school freshman and sophomore, which meant a lot more games to watch. But at least I didn't have to take her to practice. At the time, Montana allowed fifteen-year-olds who had taken drivers' education to become licensed. I often hear parents say they are nervous for their kids when they learn to drive. Frankly, I couldn't wait to squeeze out a little more time for myself.

Aside from chauffeur and fan, my primary role was to encourage her goals. Many of her friends and coaches dismissed her dream to pitch for a Division I college. No one from Montana makes it that far, some would explain. Who was she to think she could do it?

I became her advocate, countering the naysayers. "Don't listen to them. Someone's got to make it. Why *not* you?"

All of her hard work paid off, and she became a starting Division I pitcher. I was thrilled for her but lost to myself. I had devoted so much emotional energy to her goals, and once she left, I didn't have a purpose.

I once gave a talk at my Toastmasters speaking group about how Alex's determination drove her to success. My evaluator thought the speech was inspiring, but he wanted to know how Alex's story had motivated me to pursue my goals. I didn't have an answer.

All parents must go through this overidentification with their children's well-being. Single parents especially overcompensate to give their children everything they are missing from being raised by one parent.

As a single parent, I learned how to truly love another person. I gave without expectation and set aside personal desires for the well-being of another. Yet in the process, I forgot about loving myself.

Less than an hour into the Bordeaux trip, two women around my age board the train and sit directly across from me. Dressed stylishly with black shirts and square glasses, they chat while flipping through French fashion magazines. I feel embarrassed with my schlumpy appearance and turn my attention away from them. The train starts up again, and out the window I notice green grass, all variety of trees, and industrial-looking brick buildings. The scenes become blurry like an impressionist painting as the train picks up speed through the picturesque countryside.

The whirring of the train and the relaxing views make me feel sleepy. It's two in the afternoon here—but only seven in the morning back home. I don't want to sleep now and stay awake all night. Leaving behind the French vogue ladies, I walk to the dining car. On the menu I recognize the words *jambon* and *fromage* as ham and cheese in a sandwich called a *croque-monsieur*. I order the sandwich with a half-bottle of Beaujolais wine. Not the greatest French red wine, but this is a train after all. When the sandwich arrives, I realize I'm not in America anymore. Instead of the flat grilled sandwich common back home, this one comes with ham and gruyère cheese stuffed between two slices of crusty white bread and then an even thicker layer of cheese caramelized over the top slice. It's like eating pizza without the tomato sauce. Following lunch, I return to my seat and despite my intention to stay awake, I nap.

After a four-and-a-half-hour train ride, we arrive in Bordeaux. Leaving the depot becomes my first challenge, which requires me to go beneath the tracks using a ramp. On the other side, up again, but there is no ramp—only an escalator. How do people in wheelchairs survive in France? By now I'm an expert at hauling my awkward luggage. How quickly I've learned, just as I learned to manage my load as a single parent back home.

I make two trips. First, I leave my two suitcases on the bottom of the escalator and haul my bike case to the top. Then I return for my suitcases while my bike case remains unattended. My triceps and shoulders ache from the effort and I'm dripping wet. Paris was hot; Bordeaux is even hotter.

"Excusez-moi," I say loudly as I attempt to avoid ramming my suitcases into people. No one in the dense crowd offers help, and I expect none. Once outside, I sigh with relief. My hotel lies only a few blocks away. But when I come to a narrow sidewalk of crumbled bricks, again my wheels stall. Every few steps, my suitcases topple over.

I want to stop, sit down on the bricks, and cry. I stumble forward anyway. A man passing me on the sidewalk sees my predicament. He doesn't speak English, but he gestures that he will take my bike case.

Strange—it never occurs to me to ask for assistance. A single, independent woman shouldn't have to rely on anyone; I can do it on my own. Yet this time,

I'm grateful for some help. I'm so relieved as the man follows behind with my bike case and rolls it into the hotel lobby.

"*Merci beaucoup,*" I say for the second time today and wave as he leaves.

The hotel in Bordeaux looks drab with traffic-worn carpet, stained furniture, and a counter made of wood paneling and Formica. The clerk speaks English and understands when I explain that I plan to stay an extra night and use my Visa to pay. The tour group doesn't meet until tomorrow, but I chose to arrive a day early to adjust to the time change.

On my way to the elevator, I see a vending machine. I insert the euro coins that I exchanged at my bank back home and choose an orange drink. I expect Sunkist orange soda but instead taste a fizz-less, over-sweetened drink. But thirst overcomes pickiness, and I take a seat on the threadbare couch in the lobby and let the cool liquid soothe my parched throat.

The small hotel elevator means two trips to transport my luggage. On the second floor, the hallway is dark. As soon as I start moving, the lights switch on—motion-activated, obviously designed to save electricity. I don't think they are trying to be energy conscious. This is just a cheap hotel.

Two men and a woman are watching as I walk to my room.

"Are you part of the tour group?" asks a man with a British accent. I guess him to be around twenty-five.

No, I want to say. *I always lug a bike case around on my travels.* I manage a smile instead. "Yes, I am."

"I'm David," says the young man, extending his hand. "This is my wife, Kate." She has blond, curly hair, a wide smile, and looks around David's age.

The second man I presume to be in his sixties with his weathered skin and gray hair. He introduces himself as Ian from Australia. The trio tells me that they have planned to dine together, and they invite me to join them. We agree to meet in an hour, giving me time to shower and change. Goodbye frumpy sweat lady, *bonjour* French traveler.

I meet my cycling companions at an outdoor bar next to the hotel. We chat, and I accustom myself to the different rhythms of their speech. David and Kate's British accent is easy to understand. They are newlyweds on their first cycling tour together.

"David is the cyclist," Kate tells me.

David looks active and lean with a muscular build, contrasting with Kate's soft, round, plump physique. I wonder what motivated her to attempt to ride across France. Maybe she is there because her husband wants her to ride. It makes me curious if other single women will be on the tour.

Ian has a bit of a gut and doesn't strike me as a cyclist either. I strain to understand his Australian accent. It's not so much his pronunciation but the way his pitch rises and falls as he speaks.

He's curious to know more about me.

"So, Nancy…" (The way he says "Nancy" sounds almost melodic.) "You're on tour by yourself?"

"Yes. Just me."

"You're single?" Ian leans across the table, coming a little closer.

"Single and not looking." I sip my wine and turn my head, feigning interest in some people crossing the street. Then I turn my attention back to Ian. "Dating hasn't worked out so well." I want to change the subject. David and Kate pretend not to be listening, but I know that they are. Maybe if I shift the focus to Ian, he'll drop the conversation.

"How about you? You're here alone."

He chuckles a little, sensing my diversion tactic. "Yes, I'm here alone, but I live with a wonderful woman."

"So why did you decide to bike across France? It's a long way from Australia."

He leans back in his chair. "Last year I had a lacrosse injury and developed deep vein thrombosis. I was told I may never walk again."

"How awful! But you proved them wrong. You're walking."

"I made up my mind in the hospital. I wouldn't just walk; I'd ride my bike in France again."

"Again?"

"I've toured with Wide Open Road before."

David hears this and chimes in. I knew he and Kate were listening. "I've been on the tour before myself."

"Yes, and he got so skinny last time," says Kate, reaching affectionately for David's hand.

"Just too much riding?" I ask.

"No, I'm a vegetarian, and during my ride through the Pyrenees, there weren't many food options."

"This time I'm going to make sure he has enough to eat," says Kate.

We finish our drinks and then take the tram to *centre ville*, or the city center of Bordeaux. The tram stops at Place de la Bourse where we see the Miroir d'Eau, which means "water mirror." There's a thin sheet of water in the large square reflecting La Bourse, the eighteenth-century stock exchange building. A continual stream of water sprays up, producing a misty background for the people, young and old, splashing shoeless in the shallow water.

We don't linger because we're on a mission to find food. We agree on pizza, which will satisfy David's vegetarian preference, but finding a place isn't easy. We stroll down the narrow streets, passing eighteenth-century Gothic cathedrals and mansions. I notice ornate statues of ethereal women atop some of the historic structures. Even though it's after seven, the summer sun still shines brightly, forming a background of cerulean sky and white clouds for the marble buildings. I really can't believe I'm here in France.

We walk down narrow streets and find several outdoor cafés, but none is acceptable. The meals are either non-vegetarian or overpriced. I decide to ask for help instead of following my usual pattern of self-reliance. Somehow it seems easier in a foreign country to rely on the support of others.

Two couples cross the street toward us, and I ask if they know of a pizza place. One of the men speaks a little English, and he deciphers my request. They walk us to an Italian restaurant two blocks away, just as if they were escorting long-lost friends.

"Did you know those people?" David asks.

"I've never seen them before in my life."

He can't believe that I pulled random people off the street for help. And what a surprise: generous assistance, even though I asked in my broken French.

Why did I insist on doing everything on my own anyway? Is it a misguided sense of pride? A need to prove myself as self-sufficient? Spurning help has become a habit. I've become accustomed to suffering through my struggles rather than appearing weak. I could mow my own lawn, shovel my own snow, and raise my daughter by myself. This first day in France, I've discovered that people are there for me—and probably have been all along back home. I just need to extend myself and ask for help. I vow to remember this lesson during my sojourn in France—and throughout my life.

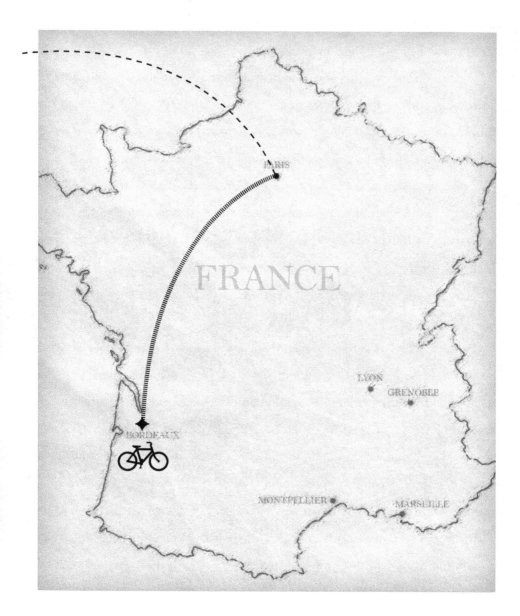

ROUTE NOTES: *Cycle through Bordeaux. See the vineyards and drink Bordeaux wine.*

DISTANCE: *40 miles or 64 kilometers*

Chapter 6

FRENCH LESSONS
IN BORDEAUX

The phone rings at midnight as I lie wide awake in my hotel room. Who is calling me in France? No one back home knows the hotel where I am staying—or the phone number, for that matter.

"Hi, this is Nate," a man begins in an unfamiliar accent. Australian, maybe? "Sorry to bother you, but I'm with the tour group. I saw your name on the email saying that you were staying an extra night."

What the hell can he want at this hour?

"I was wondering if you have any kind of bike tools with you. Mine were taken at the airport, and I want to put my bike together in the morning."

Doesn't he know that you can't bring sharp metal objects through airport security?

"I have a multitool," I tell him, referring to a compact bicycle tool with hex wrenches, screw drivers, and a chain tool. "You can use it if you want—in the *morning.*" I emphasize "morning" to make sure he doesn't have ideas of stomping up to my room in the middle of the night.

"I'll call you at eight."

I hang up the phone and still can't sleep. It's midnight in Bordeaux but only four in the afternoon in Montana. I watch TV to lull myself to sleep, but listening to the French-speaking channels doesn't relax me. At two in the morning I take an Ambien.

It must have worked because I'm jolted awake by the shrill sound of the phone. I look at the clock. Eight. Nate again. I ignore the ringing and fall back to sleep. At nine, again I hear the loud *ring, ring, ring* of Nate's doggedness. I groggily answer, "I'm still sleeping," and hang up. Nate is starting to get on my nerves. His persistence reminds me of a house fly circling my head, its relentless buzzing making me want to slap it. Why in the world does this guy need his bike put together so early in the morning anyway? The tour doesn't start until tomorrow.

I roll out of bed at ten-thirty—two-thirty in the morning back home. I still feel tired, but I don't want to sleep through my first full day in France.

The hotel serves complimentary breakfast, but by the time I make it downstairs, not a morsel remains. Beside the lobby, I notice a conference room with bikes and bike cases. This must be the assembly room. I walk in and am immediately confronted by a dark-haired, stocky-built guy close to my age. He smiles, and thrusts out his hand.

"Hi, I'm Nate."

His smile reminds me of a chipmunk. Not that he has buck teeth; rather, it's the way he presses his front teeth down on his slightly curved bottom lip. Despite the smile, he's not bad looking.

Nate tells me he's a "Kiwi," a native of New Zealand. When I introduce myself he becomes animated. He points at his half-assembled bike. "Could you get your multitool?"

The man is determined—and annoying. I return to my room to retrieve the tool along with my bike.

I watch him put his bike together. When he offers to assemble mine, my opinion of him improves, slightly. While Nate works on our bikes, David, Kate, and Ian join us to assemble theirs.

"Who wants to go for a ride?" Nate asks once our bicycles are ready.

The others have already made plans for sightseeing and relaxing. After three inactive days, I have begun to suffer bike withdrawals. Seeing my assembled bike gives me the tingle of anticipation, just like an addict scoring her drug of choice. I need a fix—a day in the saddle.

Bordeaux proves to be a biker-friendly city. Nate and I ride through town on well-marked and extensive bike lanes. Instead of the honks and dirty looks I occasionally see back home, the drivers seem courteous, welcoming even. Two young men in a car shout out, "Tour de France!" as we pedal by.

"Why would they say that?" I ask Nate.

"It's the start of the Tour today."

At our pedestrian pace, saying "Tour de France" to us is like shouting "Indy 500" to a van driver through a school zone. Maybe we look faster than I think.

Our first ten miles consist of stops and starts as we encounter many traffic lights through the city. I also have to stop for a desperate hygiene need: a razor. Among my abundant personal items, that's one necessity I forgot—and I really don't want armpit hair poking out of my bike jersey.

In pursuit of smooth armpits, I find a general store, and I ask the clerk for *un shaver*. Did I mention my French is abysmal? He doesn't understand me. I demonstrate shaving my face. He thinks I'm smoothing my hair, and he gestures to hairbrushes. Then I exhibit shaving my underarms. He consults with the people in line, and someone says, *"Un rasoir."* The clerk doesn't smile when he picks up the intercom to ask for someone to help me. What is he saying? I imagine something like, "There's a woman up front with hairy armpits in need of help." A female clerk arrives who refrains from smirking. She leads me to the back of the store to some disposable Bic razors. *Parfait.*

Speaking of hairy armpits, I've often heard Americans say that French women don't shave their underarms. This is not true, at least not today. The stereotype likely began during World War II when American servicemen were cavorting with women in France. Maybe it wasn't a cultural norm back then—or perhaps, since they had been under occupation by the Germans, shaving was the last thing on their minds.

I've often wondered why society expects women to shave underarms but not men. As it turns out, we owe smooth armpits to savvy marketing. In 1915, an exuberant young marketer working for a blade company began an advertising campaign to persuade North American women to shave their underarm hair because it was "unhygienic" and "unfeminine." It worked. In two years, his company doubled its blade sales. This new norm eventually became a standard in other parts of the world.

Walking back outside, I show my bright orange packet of razors to Nate. He doesn't seem impressed. He just shrugs and mounts his bike. Nate isn't the most expressive companion, but he rides well.

Several miles down the road, Nate and I leave the urban area and come upon a rural road. It looks like a landscape from the States. The countryside surprises me with rows of corn, pine trees, and pastures. We turn around after twenty miles since we had agreed to ride only forty for the day.

A few miles from the turnaround, Nate suggests we break for lunch when we spot a restaurant. I am famished, as my breakfast consisted of a protein bar brought from home. The restaurant has only one menu selection: steak and fries. That sounds too heavy, so we walk to a grocer next door, where I buy some bananas and peaches. Outside at the curb, I sit down and take a peach out of the paper bag. The peach looks perfect: large, soft, and speckled with subtle shades of orange and red. As I bring the fruit to my mouth, I can already smell the sweet nectar. My teeth rip through the tangy membrane. It tastes tropical, like mango but with a citrus zing. Peach juice trickles down my chin, and I wipe the drippings with my hands in between bites. Who knew France had such delectable peaches?

It's funny to me now that I didn't even like peaches until my mid-thirties when I visited my friend, Glen, in Washington. The only peaches I had known growing up were the pulpy, rock-hard ones in the produce isle or the sugary canned variety. With one bite of a Washington peach, I was in love. Peaches are now my favorite fruit, but only if they are juicy, ripe, and sweet.

The phrase *"J'ai la pêche!"* comes to mind, taught to me by a Frenchman I met in an online chat room. It literally translates to "I have the peach!" But it means so much more. When you have the peach, you are on the top of your game and feeling unstoppable. I don't have the peach yet, but maybe if I'm here long enough, I'll find it.

After lunch, we fly back to Bordeaux, thanks to a tail wind and slight descent. Nate leads the way, and I draft behind him. As we enter *centre ville*, Nate invites me to stop for a drink. As we ride around looking for a bar, we notice crowds and police. The uproar sounds like a riot, but we soon realize it's a gay pride parade. We find an outside table at a pub, order drinks, and watch the floats and marchers pass by. The participants are cheerful and flamboyantly dressed. Sound blares from car speakers and marchers with whistles.

Both Nate and I take pictures of the spectacle. A car featuring two gorgeous women—whom we believe to be cross-dressing men—parades by us. One of the participants is a very tall redhead wearing a halter-style scarlet dress that shows off endless legs. The other, a perky brunette, wears a short black dress and pink boa wrapped around the neck. I wish my legs looked as long, lean, and sexy as theirs.

A man walking by hands us our own whistles. I join in the festive spirit and begin blowing mine, copying everyone else: two long toots and three short toots. *Tooooooooot-tooooooooot-toot-toot-toot.* Nate places his whistle on the table and looks down. He appears awkward at my involvement. Maybe he feels embarrassed that participating will make him seem gay.

That evening, the entire tour group meets at a bar near the hotel. We meet the people who will be our companions for the next two weeks.

There are thirteen people in our group: four crew members and nine paying customers. The crew is led by Drew, a cherub-looking Aussie. He seems to be the ambassador of the group, chatting up everyone to make them feel welcome. Other crew members include Ellie and Jack, also Aussies, who apparently are dating based on how touchy they are with each other. Beth, an American from the West and the only other single woman, rounds out the crew.

Among the paying customers are two British couples: David and Kate and Keith and Jenny. While David and Kate are talkative, Keith and Jenny seem reserved. The rest of the customers, aside from me, are men. Nate is the lone Kiwi, and I notice that he seems quiet now that he's with a group. Simon is British and in his late twenties, I'd guess. He has a long face and nose, giving him a haughty appearance. Ian and Robbie are Aussies, and I'm drawn to both of them as people. Ian's voice and eyes twinkle as he talks, and he does talk a lot. Robbie is a native of England who moved down under to Australia. He's thin with olive skin, jet black hair, a thick moustache, and a perma-grin on his face. He reminds me of a happy version of Klinger from *M*A*S*H*.

I order a *vin rouge* (red wine) and listen to the conversation of my new friends. They discuss their lives back home—their jobs, the weather, and the soccer teams. Frankly, I don't know how to contribute to the conversation. I'm not familiar with their countries or their sports. So I listen as I sip my wine. After two hours, I'm weary of their banter. I say goodnight and go inside the bar to pay for my wine.

There's not much going on inside. I notice the only customer, a small man with thinning hair sitting on a stool. His elbows are propped on the bar and his cheeks rest on his hands. He looks like he's drunk and trying to hold his head up. The trim waitress scurries by with her tray of drinks for the outside patrons. Behind the mahogany bar is a large man with lots of dark hair. The hair flows in waves on his head and creates a shag effect on his chest. He seems proud of his carpet, wearing a white shirt that's unbuttoned to mid-chest. A gold chain with a crucifix sinks into the rug.

I walk up to the bartender and attempt to tell him that I'd like to pay for my drink. He shakes his head and corrects my French.

He's annoyed, and I'm amused. I hand him my euros and go back to the table to retrieve my camera. When I return to the bar, I imagine him thinking, "Now what does she want?" His mouth turns down, and a furrow creeps between his eyes.

"Une photo à vous, si vous plaît," I say.

"Ce n'est pas 'à vous.' C'est 'de vous,'" he corrects my French.

"Je voudrais une photo de vous, si vous plaît." I repeat, this time emphasizing the *de*.

He pauses, looking me in the eye for a moment. I grin, trying to win him over.

"D'accord," he consents.

His once gruff face softens with a broad smile.

I snap his photo and extend my hand. *"Je m'appelle Nancy. Et vous?"*

"Patrick," he tells me his name, which he pronounces "paw-TREEK."

"Je voudrais pour vous être mon professeur de français."

He laughs at the thought of being my French professor. I sit at the bar, and he conducts my lesson. He says the words and I repeat. He corrects my pronunciation, and I'm reminded of my first college French professor. Her most memorable tip: "You say the *r* by growling like a little French poodle."

Patrick doesn't provide such instruction, and after a while, he forgets about the lesson and invites me to join him for a drink. I ask for a *vin rouge*. He pours himself a shot of rum.

In America, I'm great at talking. I even attend Toastmasters once a week to practice my speaking. In France, my limited language skills mean I must focus on listening to comprehend. Patrick talks about the war in Iraq, the problems with the U.S. economy, and the Latin roots of the French language. I don't understand half of the words he says, but I do get the gist of what he means. When I clearly miss a key point, I ask for clarification from the bar waitress, who speaks some English. The difficulty of translation means my undivided attention and focus.

After an hour of listening to his monologue, Patrick seems to consider me his friend. He wants me to have another glass of wine and stay awhile. I decline and say, *"Au revoir."* With a fifty-five-mile ride in the morning, I need some sleep tonight.

As I return to my room, I wash out the day's cycling clothes. With all of the stuff I brought, I still have to keep up on laundry so I don't run out of workout wear. I think about my cycling group outside, swapping stories of home and each other's countries. They are missing out on discovering the culture right before them if they would only extend themselves, however awkwardly, to a French person.

Though I know I will welcome friends on the tour, I wonder if spending time with English-speaking comrades will limit my immersion into a French experience. I decide to avoid becoming too reliant on the comfort of the group.

During my day in Bordeaux I've learned some key life lessons. Listen more and talk less. Plunge wholeheartedly into each day's experience. Let go of the comfort of the familiar life. Pack even lighter and wash more often.

FRENCH WINE FACTS

- As a nation, the French consume more wine than any other country.
- Wine making in France began in the sixth century B.C. when Greek colonists settled in the area known today as southern France.
- Except for Spain, France has more land dedicated to vineyards than any other country.
- French vintners produce seven to eight billion bottles of wine each year.
- France and Italy vie for the title of world's largest wine producer.
- While American wines are commonly labeled based on the grape used, French wines are distinguished by the area where the grapes are grown and the wine is made.
- Wines receive classification through the *appellation d'origine contrôlée* (AOC), which certifies the grape varieties and wine-making practices that must be used in each of the wine regions.
- The ten principal wine-growing regions of France are Alsace, Bordeaux, Burgundy, Champagne, Côtes du Rhône, Languedoc-Roussillon, Loire Valley, Provence, Corsica, and South West.

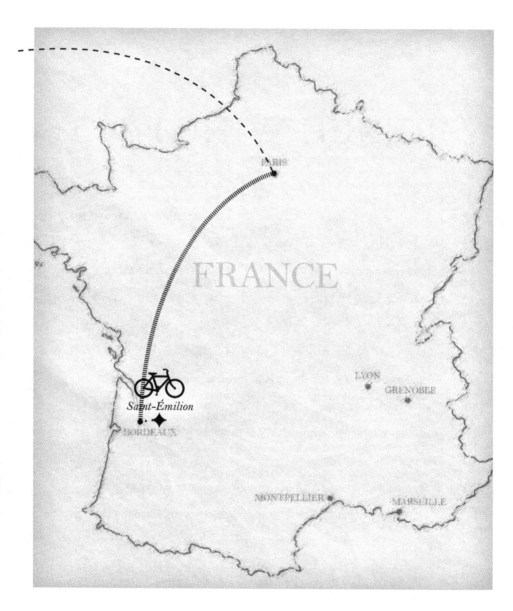

ROUTE NOTES: *Cycle from Bordeaux to Saint-Émilion, with lunch at Cadillac.*
Area is famous for Saint-Émilion wine (blending Merlot, Cabernet Franc and
sometimes a bit of Cabernet Sauvignon) and macaroons.

DISTANCE: *55 miles or 89 kilometers*

Chapter 7

FALLING INTO
WINE COUNTRY

We look like long-time friends as we gather for pictures before our first day of riding. In truth, we're strangers who met as cycling companions through Internet matchmaking. Our jerseys display the colors of the rainbow arching across the entrance of the hotel where we pose. Jack, our mechanic, stands next to me with his right arm around my shoulder and his left draped over the rider on his other side. David props his elbow on Ian's shoulder. We've barely met, but somehow our pending adventure encourages a familiarity that otherwise would not exist.

Drew hands each of us a map for the day. Ellie has taped plastic sheaths to our bike handlebars in which we can insert our maps. We will ride to Cadillac (pronounced "cah-dee-YAHK") for lunch and then on to Saint-Émilion for the night. Ellie pulls away in the support van carrying our luggage. Everyone else rides as a group leaving town. After a few miles, I find the pace agonizingly slow. I pick up speed, and Nate sticks with me.

I feel invigorated and joyful as I pedal through the countryside. I'm really in France riding my bike. I see the first wine shop.

"Let's stop," I call to Nate who is behind me.

Nate pulls over with me. We walk inside, and a woman sets up samples for us. I taste the wine while Nate stands and watches.

"This isn't bad. Do you want to try some?" I ask.

"No, I don't really like wine."

"How can you not like wine?"

"Don't know. I just don't."

Seriously? He's in France. The *heart* of wine country. Billions of grapes are grown in this region, which will be fermented into more than 700 million bottles to be imported the world over. This is the wine capital of the world! And he doesn't feel like trying some? What a putz.

"Well, I like it," I say and down my next sample.

I walk over to the shelf to check out the price for a bottle. It's amazingly cheap, only three to four euros for a bottle. The two men and one woman who work at the store huddle nearby, watching me.

"Excusez-moi. Je voudrais du vin pour moi."

They nod, happy I want their wine. The woman starts walking over to the cash register to ring up my purchase. I can't stash a bottle of wine in my back jersey pocket.

"How do I say, 'Ship it to the United States'?" I ask Nate.

"Don't ask me. I don't speak French."

I smile at the store clerks. *"Je suis américaine. Je voudrais votre vin aux États-Unis."*

As I literally tell them I want their wine in the United States, they look puzzled. They obviously don't understand. They respond in French. Now *I* don't understand. I try again, combining new words, focusing on my pronunciation. How do I say *mail* or *transport* in French? As I struggle with the right words, I see Beth walk in.

"Everything OK?" she asks, smiling at Nate and me. She must think that we're having a romantic rendezvous in the wine shop. Oh, well.

"We're just wine tasting," I explain, although I'm the only one surrounded by wine glasses. I tell Beth of my predicament.

She talks to the clerks in French, and they shake their heads.

"They can't ship the wine," she tells me. "I wouldn't worry. Much better wine is to come."

Beth looks at me and then Nate again, and gives another knowing smile. "Have a nice ride," she says as she leaves the store.

The wine clerks are staring, waiting for me to either buy wine or leave. I can only imagine what they think of me, dressed for cycling, glugging their samples, and babbling in American Franglais. I feel half foolish, half guilty, and I know it's time to go. We bid farewell to the shop clerks and return to our bikes.

Onward to Cadillac we pedal. We pass through several villages along the way and stop to pose in front of an old church. Nate uses my camera to snap a photo of me with my bike. Then I take one of him with his camera.

"OK. Let's go," I say.

"Just a minute. I want to take some more photos."

It's nice that he can ride well and take time to appreciate his surroundings. I don't mind waiting. I watch him ride to the side of the church and see him take out his camera. I stand straddling my bike and pull out my map to study the route ahead. When I look up, Nate has disappeared.

Where did he go?

Five minutes pass. He doesn't return.

Maybe he has ridden off without me. My earlier poor opinion of him returns. I continue alone through the village and up a hill. Reaching the summit, I see an old cemetery. Curious, I pass through the gate, then set my bike down and walk over to read the tombstones. Many of the stones are crumbled, and dates on the older ones are difficult to read. A balding man in his late fifties walks toward me.

"Bonjour," I say.

He returns my greeting, and in my awkward French, I tell him I'm an American on a cycling holiday. Bord—as in Bordeaux—is visiting his cousin's grave. Like Patrick the day before, Bord talks politics with me. He can't understand the war and why the American people elected George Bush—twice. He thinks the first President Bush was fine, but this one—and the war—are *"très terrible."* Why do the French always want to talk politics, especially with me? I'm one of the least political people I know.

Enough with the politics—I'm here to ride. I say goodbye to Bord and jump on my bicycle. The bright sun, cloudless sky, and moderate temperatures make the day perfect for riding. I'm savoring the tranquility and stillness of the French countryside. I realize I don't miss Nate; I'm completely content on my own. And I feel so strong today that I think I have *la pêche.* I look down at my Cateye computer and see I'm speeding along at twenty-two miles per hour. The day, my ride, is perfection. I'm lost in my reverie when my attention abruptly shifts back to the road.

CLANK.

What was that? Did something fall off? Did I run over something?

Panic causes an instinctive reaction. I slam on my back brake, and my bike fishtails. I'm going to crash. Time slows as I assess possible landing places. To the right, a ravine with a concrete embankment. I'll flip over if I hit the barrier. Ahead, a gravel driveway. I steer my handlebars in that direction. My bike skids sideways on the red rocks. I'm falling over. My knee and elbow land first. Then my body slides along the gravel before coming to a stop. I lie silently for a few seconds. I notice a car inching forward toward me. It stops. A woman emerges and walks over to me. How embarrassing that she saw my fall. I hurriedly lift the bicycle off me and stand up. Good. My bike isn't hurt. My body didn't fare as well. A road rash covers my right knee and shin and my right elbow drips blood.

The woman is standing by me now and says something in French. I'm too distracted to focus on her words.

"Je ne comprends pas." I don't understand what she means.

Come with me, she motions. This must be her driveway, her house. Before following her, I walk down the road to where the clank happened. My rear light fell off. I pick up the plastic pieces and then trail the lady into her home.

She appears to be in her early forties and typifies my idea of a French woman. Her dark hair is stylishly cropped, her big brown doe eyes are accentuated with smoky eye shadow, and her full lips are glossed in pink. She's dressed in a sexy, low-cut black shirt and tight-fitting jeans. Inside, there's a man who doesn't seem so concerned with appearance. He wears a white Beefy-T and Levi's. I assume this is her husband. He speaks to the woman in French, too rapidly for me to understand, likely asking who I am and what happened. What can she say? "This crazy American cyclist skidded into our driveway right as I was turning into it."

Neither of them speaks English, but the woman and I communicate through my bit of French and the universal language of gesturing. She points to the sink and indicates that I should wash my wounds. Meanwhile, she takes out her comprehensive first aid kit from a kitchen cupboard. She sprays on antiseptic that stings and stains my skin yellow. Then she swathes a bandage around the cut on my elbow, holding it in place with fishnet gauze. She places two tablets in my hand, pain relievers I assume, and pours me a glass of water to wash them down.

"Je m'appelle Nancy," I tell her and ask for her name.

"Ah-HOR-ha," she says in a very French way.

"Pardonnez?"

"Ah-HOR-ha," she repeats.

I ask her to spell the name.

"A-U-R-O-R-A."

"Comme la constellation?" I don't know how to say "Northern Lights" in French.

"Oui!" she says and smiles, delighted I understand.

What a strange pronunciation for such a beautiful name.

The aroma of roasted meat and vegetables reminds me it's lunchtime. I'm hungry, and I'd enjoy eating with this French family—Aurora, her husband, and their nine- or ten-year-old son who has walked into the kitchen. But they don't invite me, and I don't ask. Besides, I have to meet up with the group for lunch. I thank Aurora, my charming guardian angel and head out the door. As I ride, my scrapes and cuts hurt a little. Mostly I'm humiliated that I slammed on my brakes and fell—a beginner's error. When I arrive in Cadillac, I see some tour group riders relaxing outside at a crêpe restaurant.

"What happened to you?" David asks, seeing my bandaged arm.

I admit my stupidity at slamming on my brakes.

"We wondered when Nate showed up before you," Kate says. As if on cue, Nate strolls over to our table.

"Where did you go?" Nate chimes in, as if I was the one who vanished.

"I couldn't find you. So I left."

"I told you I was taking photos. When I came back, I saw you riding up the hill, and then you disappeared." That must have been when I turned into the cemetery.

I can hear concern in his voice. But still, he must have ridden off somewhere; otherwise, I would have seen him. I'm still annoyed, so I decide to distance myself from him.

We sit outdoors, and I order a ham and cheese crêpe and some house Bordeaux wine. I need a drink after the fall. Surprisingly, even the house wine is excellent. While I sip wine and wait for my crêpe, I notice a gray-haired man with black-rimmed glasses. He stands by the shop next door leaning against a sign with a cartoon pig that announces the specials. I walk over, point at the sign and say, "Piggy." He laughs.

I tell him I'd like his photo. He agrees, and hugs and kisses the pig sign as I take the picture.

We introduce ourselves. His name is Joel (pronounced "zho-ELL"). He speaks no English, but with my improving French—from incomprehensible to poor—he and I communicate. Across from us is a monument that says *Centre de Resistance*. I ask Joel why such a sleepy village would possess this claim. Joel says that it's a memorial for people who died in World War II. He walks me to the monument so I can inspect it closer. Then he asks me to follow him, and we walk along a narrow medieval street the width of an alley. Where is he taking me? A half a block down the road, he points out a plaque embedded into bricks on the street. It says the town was formed in the thirteenth century. Joel explains that Cadillac had fought for independence against England in the Hundred Years' War (which ironically lasted more than a hundred years).

Of course, the name Cadillac is common in the U.S. Most people don't know that the famous automobile line was named after seventeenth-century French explorer Antoine de la Mothe, sieur de Cadillac, who founded Detroit, Michigan. He was born ninety miles south of the town of Cadillac in Saint-Nicolas-de-la-Grave. Though the names are the same, one would never associate the quaint petite village with the lavish oversized automobile. I wonder why Antoine would ever leave lush and beautiful southwestern France to found a city in America's bitter cold interior. Somehow I can't picture someone like Joel enjoying Motown.

After lunch, we travel nearly thirty miles to our camping spot near Saint-Émilion. Most of the way, I ride with Nate and Simon, who move along at a good clip. The three of us pass through villages and vineyards without conversing. The towns have names that I practice pronouncing as I ride along—Sauveterre, Mourens, Gornac, Coirac, Rauzan.

In between towns are signs for Château de this or Château de that—wineries of the Bordeaux region. Old villages, colorful flowers, and the fertile green hills of vineyards delight my senses.

Simon and Nate are better climbers, and they drop me riding the hill into Saint-Émilion. As I enter the village on my own, I spot their bikes at a bar. I walk inside and see the two sitting at a table.

"Do you want a drink?" asks Simon. I'm surprised he's offering to buy. He really hasn't said more than a few sentences to me since we met, except to correct my French.

"Sure, some red wine would be great. Thanks."

I sit down at their table and watch the Tour de France live on television. I had thought I was making improvements in my French comprehension, but listening to the rapid chatter of the announcers, I realize that my vocabulary needs work. The only word I consistently pick up is *peloton,* which means the pack in a bicycle race.

Simon returns with our drinks and soon the Aussie tour riders arrive at our hangout. Robbie pulls up a chair next to me.

"How was your ride, Nance?" he asks.

"Great. How was yours?"

"Ah, couldn't been better. It was a lovely day."

I have the feeling that every day would be lovely through Robbie's eyes. He just seems an eternal optimist.

Robbie turns his attention to the TV. His Australian countryman Cadel Evans is a favorite to win the Tour de France. However, on today's flat course the stage win goes to one of the sprinters.

Following our afternoon break, we're back on our bikes climbing a steep hill toward our campground, which really isn't the right word for this place. It's more like a resort with tents, complete with showers, a restaurant, pool, washer and dryer, and Internet access. I pitch my tent, unpack my sleeping pad and sleeping bag, and then shower and dress in sweats. I didn't realize that we had a group meal in town, so when the taxi shuttle comes, I don't have time to change out of my athletic pants. Ironic that last night I had prided my transformation to classy French tourist, and now frumpy sweat lady returns.

Saint-Émilion is an eighth-century walled village built on undulating hills. Limestone buildings in shades of beige and gray line the cobblestone streets. Drew tells us that Saint-Émilion is famous for macaroons and fine wine. The village claims to be the birthplace of the macaroon, the simple almond biscuit first made here in the seventeenth century by nuns who lived in a local convent. I'm more interested in the wine of Saint-Émilion. When we arrive, I follow the crew members and Nate into a wine shop. The sommelier, James, is a Brit expatriate. He lines up glasses of different wines for us to taste, explaining that the red wines of the region blend Merlot, Cabernet Franc, and sometimes a bit of Cabernet Sauvignon. James encourages us to guess the percentage of the different grapes used in each bottle, and Ellie and Beth seem excited to play this game. I quietly sip the samples, not caring about the subtle nuances. Beth was right—these wines are much better.

We finish our tasting and walk outside the shop, where the village of Saint-Émilion has taken on a glow. I breathe in the essence of the place. From my vantage point perched high above the village, I see that the brownish-gray stone rooftop shingles now reflect a pinkish hue. With its crooked streets and old houses, Saint-Émilion reminds me of the village in the movie *Chocolat*. The evening light must have inspired the artist standing next to me who is painting the scene below. I snap his photo, but he doesn't look my way. His focus only vacillates between the canvas and the softly lit village.

Drew points down to the outdoor tables where we will dine, and we descend steep rock steps to the restaurant. For the next several hours we enjoy a five-course dinner washed down with several glasses of wine.

Ian sits across from me, and he continues to probe me about my dating. Everyone else is talking, and they don't seem to pay attention.

"Things just haven't worked out for me. What more can I say?" It's not like I haven't *tried* dating.

"Maybe you just haven't met the right person."

"I thought I had."

Dante seemed so right. He was a good-looking biker and doctor who was so fun to be around. But it was more than that: I admired his ambition, adventurous spirit, and sense of humor. He was probably the only man I ever dated who wasn't intimidated by my confidence and success in my work. Maybe that's why I had fallen for him.

"If he was the right person, you'd know it," says Ian.

"But what if the problem is me? Maybe I'm just too difficult, too particular, and not considerate enough."

"That's just nonsense, Nancy. If all these blokes don't appreciate you, then they don't deserve you."

Ian's words make me feel better. I never thought a man in his sixties would be my dating confidant. Yes, maybe *they* don't deserve *me*. Usually, it's me chastising myself for all of my shortcomings. Not that I feel relieved of my flaws, but Ian is pointing out that the right guy would appreciate me, even with my imperfections.

Could that have been my problem all along? Not the rejection by others, but the rejection of myself? Deep down, maybe I don't feel worthy to be loved. If I just do enough, achieve enough, improve myself enough, then maybe someone will finally accept me. Of course, it never works that way.

I think it's like in the movie *Bridget Jones' Diary*. Like many women, Bridget thinks the answer is to be more beautiful and interesting, or at least thinner. Then she meets Mark Darcy who tells her, "I like you just as you are." Bridget is dumbfounded. She can't believe that someone can accept her just as she is: a plump smoker who sometimes drinks too much.

While the central message of the movie is about finding love, I think a subtler theme is that to find love, we have to learn to accept ourselves. If we don't like ourselves just as we are, we won't believe that anyone else can appreciate us.

I'm not one who likes to dwell on the past, especially not my childhood. But I will admit that feeling unworthy of love stems from those early years. I was raised the youngest of five children to parents who rarely showed affection to me, my siblings, or each other. My dad liked to yell, and many times my mother would be the object of his outbursts. He'd tell her how dumb she was, unworthy to do anything more than take care of a house. Mostly, she'd just take his verbal abuse or remove herself from his presence. When I was around fourteen, my mother moved out of the house for a few weeks. She would come home during the day when my dad was gone to clean and cook us meals.

"Why don't you leave?" I asked her once when I visited her at the cheap hotel where she was staying.

"I have you to take care of," she said. "And besides, I have to wait for my pension."

Mother didn't work, but she knew if she bided her time, she would receive her own pension as a spouse of a railroad worker. Eventually she came home, moving into her own bedroom. My parents lived separate lives in the same house after that.

My upbringing taught me that I never wanted to be in her situation, forced to stay with a man for financial reasons. I'd earn a college degree, establish a career—and never depend on anyone. This internal drive for self-sufficiency helped me to achieve a degree of worldly success, but it didn't comfort a heart that longed to be loved. For a dating woman over forty, success created more barriers. The same toughness that helped me thrive in life created walls in relationships for most men—but not for Dante. Even though things didn't work out between us, he was never intimidated by my success, drive, or ambition. And I appreciated that he accepted me.

When the shuttle meets us, I'm exhausted from the day, from the conversation, and from the wine. I'm ready for my first night of camping. When my daughter was younger, she and I camped frequently. Our last camping trip happened nine years before, and I haven't been in a tent since. But while I remember our gigantic orange tent as spacious, my new bargain-priced Walmart tent is tiny. I had considered bringing "Orange Jumbo" to France, but then I had second thoughts. It wouldn't fit into my suitcase, and even if it had, I thought setting up a circus-sized tent might make me the laughingstock of the campground.

The packaging claimed that the Walmart tent was six feet long. This is a lie. I've placed my sleeping pad across the longest part of the tent, and I can't fully stretch out my five-foot-eight-inch frame. My large suitcase rests beside my legs with the backpack on top. My small suitcase lies near my head. Everything—including me—is crammed inside.

I sleep restlessly on the rock-hard sleeping pad. My discomfort and the snoring, coughing, and farting noises from the camping cyclists keep waking me. How can I survive two weeks of this? I shift around, trying to drown out the sounds and find a comfortable position. By three in the morning I can't take it anymore. I let some air out of the sleeping pad and pop an Ambien. I'm stiff, sore, and tired. I sure miss the shabby Bordeaux hotel.

Patched up after my fall.

Chapter 8

A BIRTHDAY
IN THE VINEYARDS

My last trip to the vineyards happened when I turned forty. While this seemed like a magnificent way to spend my birthday, touring wineries was admittedly my second choice. I first envisioned a romantic escape with my then boyfriend, Jim, but he claimed work demands precluded a weekend getaway with me. How could I have known that "work" included his on-the-side girlfriend?

So I called one of my best friends, Glen, who agreed to play host as I crossed the boundary into the unknown world of forty. His home in Washington's Columbia Valley would serve as the base for my solo jaunts to the area's wineries.

On the last day of my thirty-ninth year, I began my winery tour near the town of Peshastin. Down a gravel road lined with apple and pear trees, I found my first stop: the Icicle Ridge Winery.

A grand log home beckoned, but when I stepped up to the door a sign read "Closed." Disappointed, I climbed back into my SUV and backtracked. As I reached the main road, I noticed another sign, one I hadn't seen before: "Wine Grapes." I pulled over and walked toward the sign. It was mid-October, and large grape leaves were painted in fall colors—yellow, orange, and caramel. Succulent purple grapes hung heavily on the vines pleading to be picked. Beside the sign a wooden bench invited me to sit awhile.

I plucked some grapes off the vine and popped them one by one into my mouth. These were the sweetest, juiciest grapes I had ever tasted, making table grapes seem sour and pulpy in comparison.

As I relaxed, I pulled out my journal to capture my thoughts. Perched on a hill that overlooked the valley below, I saw the Wenatchee River. Beside the river, traffic rushed along Highway 2, creating a hectic contrast to the peaceful scene.

What a relief to observe the chaos rather than participate. My life back home overflowed with the hassles of working, completing a master's in business, and raising a teenage daughter. The simple act of indulging on grapes on a bench seemed decadent. It almost made me feel a little guilty to be so aimless. There I was with no agenda, totally free to do what I wanted, where I wanted, when I wanted—at least for the weekend. And right then, I only wanted to sit on that bench and savor sweet grapes.

My reverie was interrupted by an old blue pickup rumbling from the winery down the gravel road. The young man driving the truck slowed as he passed and looked my way. Then he turned around and returned toward the winery.

A few minutes later, the man in the truck drove down the road again. Maybe I shouldn't have been there, but I didn't want to leave—the grapes tasted so good and relaxing in the daylight warmed my core. He looked at me again, so this time I waved. To my surprise he pulled over, rolling down his window.

"Are you from the newspaper?" he asked.

"Newspaper? No." Discretely leaving the grapes on the bench, I walked toward the truck. I stopped near the road, a few feet away from him.

"We're waiting for a reporter and photographer. I thought you might be looking for the winery." He seemed to welcome me with his smile. He didn't appear to notice the grapes I'd left behind.

"I'm here to visit the winery. Just waiting for it to open."

"It's open now. You can go down. My wife is pouring samples."

"Great! I'll go down. I'm Nancy, by the way." I walked closer to the pickup to extend my hand to him.

"Nice to meet you. I'm Glenn." Then he told me his last name.

"What did you say your name was?"

He repeated his name.

I was surprised because my friend, the Glen with whom I was staying, had the same exact first and last name. But this Glenn told me that he spelled his name with two *n*'s instead of one. Yet what were the odds? It seemed like a sign. A sign for what, I wasn't sure.

True confession time: I have spent lots of time looking for signs in life. I'm practical, grounded, and yet I still have this "woo woo" side that believes in signs from tarot cards, palm readings, and unexplained coincidences. I couldn't say why, but I knew this was the place I needed to be. I HAD A SIGN!

Glenn put his truck in gear and headed once again toward the winery. I followed him toward the log home. Inside, Glenn's wife poured me six samples, one at a time. The owners of the Icicle Ridge Winery, Lou and Judy, introduced themselves. They had once farmed pears and apples, but as foreign fruit had glutted the U.S. market, their viable livelihood had become precarious. The fertile Columbia Valley was transforming into a wine region, and many local farmers were embracing this new opportunity.

Within an hour, the real journalists showed up. They wanted pictures of the grape harvest, and Lou and Judy asked me to help them snip grapes off the vine. I joined the couple, another tourist, and a crew of workers out in the vineyards. With quick instructions, I was soon cutting grapes off the vine like a pro. I clipped for an hour, putting the grapes and stems into large crates, sipping red wine as I worked. If this wasn't the normal practice, then it should have been. How satisfied I was with the simplicity of harvest as the October sun warmed my face. While I worked, the newspaper photographer snapped my photo and the reporter interviewed me, asking me such important questions as why I was there (my birthday) and how I had enjoyed my day (very much, thank you).

With the grape cutting completed, I followed Judy back into the house. She thanked me for my work, hugged me, and bagged two bottles of wine for my trouble. I didn't deserve compensation, but I couldn't possibly refuse her gift, especially since it was wine. Instead, I felt that I owed this wine family for sharing their wisdom of life through wine making.

I could learn about life through wine making's rhythm. Wine needs time to season into its fullness as the aging process mellows out the harshness of the young grapes. Different varietals produce different tastes, and sometimes blending the best characteristics of each makes a smoother glass of wine. As I turned forty, wine showed me that the young and new can be sweet but simple—far better to have some age and a fullness of flavor.

Wine, like people, captures the essence of its surroundings. I recognized the flavor of apples and pears in some bottles I sampled, a reflection of the land. I could also taste the subtle differences of the oak barrels. Wines aged in American oak tended to have more of a toasty vanilla flavor. French oak released more tannin, and wine aged in these barrels had more body and astringency.

Later in the day, I visited another winery and the vintner told me that even the emotional environment affects the wine. "Wine needs quiet and love," he said. "It will not taste good if it is associated with hate." *Hate?* Who could experience hate while drinking delectable wines?

The boundary that I crossed into forty was not what I anticipated. Instead of a daunting future heading toward old age, I discovered something quite wonderful—an effortless way of being in the world. I longed for nature's rhythms where my life had a season, and I lived simply, nurtured by the environment.

Being in France brings back memories of my birthday in Washington. Earth and sky, flowers and vineyards, medieval villages and cobblestone streets help me discard remnants of my life back home and sink my soul into the beauty that surrounds me.

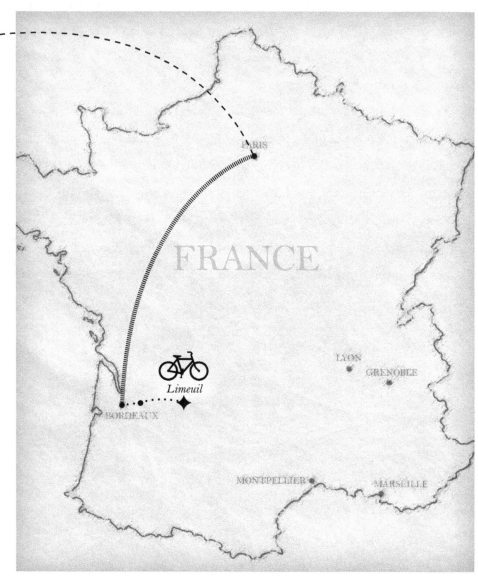

ROUTE NOTES: *Cycle through the vineyards from Saint-Émilion to Limeuil with a picnic lunch at the Château de Monbazillac. The red wines of the area include Bergerac, Côtes de Bergerac, and Pécharmant. White wines include Monbazillac, a sweet-tasting wine served as an apéritif.*

DISTANCE: *72 miles or 116 kilometers*

Chapter 9

ALONG THE DORDOGNE

Hoo hooooo hooooo. Hoo hooooo hooooo. I lie in my tent listening to the haunting coo of an unfamiliar bird. While the camper noise symphony plays throughout the night, the birds join the chorus in the morning. And one particular bird sounds like none I've heard before.

I stretch as fully as I can in my confined space. My body aches. My elbow and leg hurt from yesterday's fall. My back is stiff from sleeping on the rock-hard sleeping pad. And my right knee twinges from riding. Day two will be a long day in the saddle, around seventy miles, a daunting prospect. A cycling tour in France seemed like such a good idea, but now I'm having doubts. Can I really make it through two full weeks of biking?

Our day begins with breakfast under the canvas canopy set up by the crew: cereal, freshly cut fruit, French pastries, English tea, and coffee from a press. I fill a bowl of muesli and add fruit. I pour coffee into a plastic cup, noticing the grounds swirling around the edge. I join the others, taking a seat in one of the plastic white chairs placed in a semicircle beneath the canopy.

"I heard the strangest sounding bird this morning," I say to the cyclists and crew sitting down to eat. I imitate the sound I heard. "Does anyone know what it is?"

No one answers. Do they not know? Or do they think that such a stupid question doesn't deserve an answer? Maybe they didn't hear me.

I feel awkward being ignored. I keep quiet, sip my ground-infested coffee, and listen to the others. I notice that cliques are already forming. Obviously, the young English couples stick together: David with Kate and Keith with Jenny. Of course, the crew is a clique. But I'm also noticing that both Ian and Simon have bonded with Robbie, but not really with each other. The only outliers are Nate and me. No way will I buddy up with him. I feel somewhat isolated, but I can't let it bring me down. My goal isn't to make friends and hang out with the English-speaking tour mates anyway. I'm here to experience France.

After breakfast, I launch into pre-riding rituals. I dress in my cycling gear. In the back pockets of my jersey I stash the day's necessities: camera, money, protein bar (brought from home), and jacket. Water bottles are filled—one with water and the other with sports drink (also brought from home). Next, I tear down my camping site. Hanging on tree branches is the laundry from the night before, which I retrieve and put in my small suitcase. I fold up the sleeping bag, deflate the sleeping pad, and take down the tent. These I put into my large suitcase. I wheel both of these and carry the backpack on my shoulders to the support van.

By nine, everyone is packed and we're ready to leave. Our journey will take us to Limeuil. I start with the group, and again the pace is too slow, so I surge ahead. This time Nate lags behind. He seems to want to ride slower, and I don't care.

Despite my accident, I enjoyed riding on my own yesterday. Besides, Nate seems too unpredictable.

From Saint-Émilion, our bike route follows narrow country lanes lined with vineyards. I stop at the first town I see, Saint-Christophe-des-Bardes, where a farmer's market is in full swing. I take photos and then ride slowly through the crowds. Heading toward Castillon-la-Bataille, I ride alongside the Dordogne River. I travel against the current, heading eastward while the Dordogne flows west.

High in the mountains of Auvergne above the town of Mont-Dore, the Dordogne begins at the point where two small rivers meet: the Dore and the Dogne. From there it journeys west for nearly 300 miles to just north of Bordeaux.

The Dordogne flows gently, and travel guides recommend that the best way to see the river is by kayak or canoe. I suggest traveling by bicycle on the rural back roads that run parallel to the river. The Dordogne valley is a lush region with pastoral green fields and hardwood trees flanking the river. I find myself slowing down to take in the beauty, sometimes stopping to take photos.

I've always found a sense of peace and serenity near water. My family comes from Duluth, Minnesota, which is a port city on Lake Superior. Every summer during my high school years, I would visit my Aunt Evelyn and Uncle Clarence there. Many days I'd enjoy walking along the rocky shores of Lake Superior, skipping stones and reclining on boulders while listening to the water lap the shore.

My home in south central Montana is semi-arid, and water isn't abundant like it is in Minnesota, known for its ten thousand lakes. Our only nearby water is the Yellowstone River, a river very different from the Dordogne.

While the Dordogne runs slowly and peacefully, the Yellowstone flows rapidly. The banks of the Dordogne are green and lush; the Yellowstone's are dry and sandy.

These rivers contrast, just as my life as a traveler in France differs markedly from life back home. In my "real world" I scramble from activity to activity, goal to goal, relationship to relationship, swimming against the current much of the time. I fight for shore, no matter how challenging the swim.

The irony is that I made it to shore long ago. Well, I haven't found the right guy, but I've accomplished so much in my life since my divorce. I have established a successful career, bought a home, kept physically fit, and have been blessed with good friends. Most importantly, I have provided a stable life for my daughter. Now grown, Alex thrives as a college athlete and scholar.

I don't need to struggle anymore. And yet, like the Yellowstone, I persist in rushing through my life. I leap into the water and flail against the current. This is what I know. Maybe challenging relationships are just another way for me to swim upstream.

In France, I meander, gently flowing from place to place. This is how I want life to be. I don't need anything—or anyone—to be happy. My time by the river infuses my spirit with the bliss of simply being.

Lunch today will be served picnic-style beside a castle called the Château de Monbazillac. As with most castles, it stands atop a steep hill. As I ride toward the palace, I'm forced to shift to a lower gear to make it up. My legs rebel at the exertion, so I take the climb slowly. By the time I reach the top, I'm tired and starving, but lunch isn't ready.

While I wait for food, I wander to the castle to see the structure up close. Picture a fairytale castle surrounded by vineyards, and you'll get an idea of

Château de Monbazillac. As I stroll down the long walkway toward the castle, I imagine myself as a princess back in the sixteenth century when the castle was built. I'd wear a dress with a full skirt and lots of frills around the neck. Maybe I'd peer out one of the top windows watching the horses gallop toward the castle.

There are no horses on the pathway these days, only tourists. I contemplate a look inside Château de Monbazillac, but it's already one o'clock and the English language tour isn't scheduled until three. Walking back to our picnic site, I take in the vineyards. The area grows Sémillon, Sauvignon, and Muscadelle grapes which are used for the region's sweet, honey-tasting wine appropriately named Monbazillac. Drinking wine as sugary as candy doesn't appeal to me, but apparently it's quite popular.

I return to the group and sit on a plastic chair. As I wait to eat, I notice that dark clouds have gathered in the sky and the temperature is dropping. Chilled, I take my jacket out of my back jersey pocket and put it on.

Finally, lunch is served—a picnic spread with chicken, gourmet salads, and an assortment of bread. While the others seem to relish the opportunity to enjoy a leisurely lunch and chat, I'm eager to eat quickly, hop on my bike, and outrace the rain—ready to plunge into the rapids again. With twenty-six miles left to ride, I want to arrive at camp early, tend to my chores, and get to sleep before ten.

Five minutes into my ride, the rain pours down. My water-resistant jacket keeps me dry on top, but my sunglasses become streaked with water, and my feet turn ice-cold. A tail wind pushes me along, and I surge toward the campground. I still have more than twenty miles to go; if I stop, I'll just become colder. The towns fade into a blur as I single-mindedly pedal. Just this morning I enjoyed riding slowly through the Dordogne River valley, and now I'm back to my habit of rushing through life.

By the time I arrive at the campground in Limeuil, the rain has stopped. I show up before the support van, and so I go inside the campground bar and order a glass of red wine. Soon, Drew, Ellie, and Kate show up in the van.

Kate is a paying customer, but she doesn't seem to want to ride. Yesterday, she only rode half of the route because the last part was hilly. Today's excuse was that she didn't have rain gear. Why wouldn't she bring rain gear on a two-week excursion? Is she really serious about cycling? I can't imagine her husband would pressure her to take it up. David seems fully supportive and encouraging of Kate, definitely not the pushy sort. I've even seen him slow down to accompany her which must be agony for a serious cyclist like David. Not that it's any of my business. I have enough of my own relationship issues to deal with.

When I walk over to the van to retrieve my gear, Ellie surprises me with a compliment.

"You really made good time."

"The rain gave me some extra motivation," I say, trying to feign modesty.

I appreciate the kind words. It really took a while for me to become a strong rider. I remember months of riding with the local cycling group (mostly men) and barely clinging on to the back of the pack. Inevitably, I'd be dropped from the group and would have to pedal by myself for the rest of our ride. But I kept working and pushing, and eventually I managed to stick with them. Except for uphill climbs where I still got dropped, I held my own against the other riders.

The best compliment I heard came from Coach Jay a year after I started training with him. He told me when he first met me in his wind-training class he thought there was no hope for me. He said he was surprised how strong of a cyclist I had become. With work, I could become even better. (Coach Jay ALWAYS stressed work.)

I can think of two reasons why I pushed so hard. First, I had passion for the sport. When I flew down the road on my bicycle, I felt a sense of escape, of freedom. The exertion became meditation for me. Second, my ego egged me on. Before I joined up with the cycling group, I rode with Jeff and his friends. At first I plodded along at fifteen to sixteen miles per hour—but Jeff was patient, giving me tips to improve. I persevered, torturing myself trying to hang with them. They'd leave me behind, pedaling a half mile or more up the road. I'd go as hard as possible, struggling to keep them in eyesight. I vowed that one day I would keep up with them. My opportunity came a few months later when I felt strong and rode a half-mile ahead of Jeff and friends, averaging more than twenty miles per hour.

I was thrilled that I could finally go their pace, but Jeff seemed despondent after the ride. He became quiet and went home after giving me a quick peck goodbye. His gloomy mood continued for days, according Charles, who cycled with him afterwards. Charles even told me that Jeff threw down his expensive carbon-fiber bike and said he wasn't worthy to ride it. I guess Jeff's ego needed validation, too. Maybe that's why I "bugged" him.

There's something about pushing myself that gives me great internal satisfaction. Sometimes, when there's nothing going right in a day, I look forward to charging hard down the road. I must admit that it's still gratifying to ride stronger than everyone else—like today when I beat everyone to camp, even though I started a little before the others.

It's my pattern in life to push hard and to be rewarded for my accomplishments. Maybe it's time to let go of always pushing, not just on my bike but in life. I've driven myself to advance in my career, achieve financial stability, and raise my daughter. What if I can let life's current ease me downstream to whatever waits around the next bend?

As I lie in my sleeping bag tonight, I envision myself floating on the Dordogne. Its melancholy current gently guides me, and I relax in the water, letting the river carry me along. I fall asleep with that image in my mind and sleep soundly. Even the campground symphony of noises doesn't stir me.

The River Dordonge.

The Château de Monbazillac is a sixteenth century castle
surrounded by vineyards used for the honey-tasting wine made in the area.

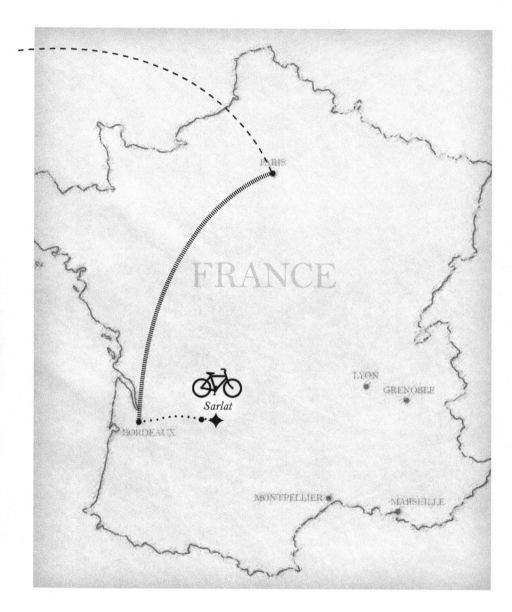

ROUTE NOTES: *Cycle from Limeuil to Sarlat through the forests of the Périgord Noir region. Chance to see a replica of a prehistoric cave. Area is known for foie gras, truffles, and nuts.*

DISTANCE: *67 miles or 108 kilometers*

Chapter 10

Les Grottes

Today, I ride out of camp and catch up with Robbie, Simon, and Ian. I decide to join them as they saunter down the road. We ride to Le Bugue, where I stop to take photos at the farmer's market. The three men continue on their way. When I start up again, I realize that the road on the map is blocked by the farmer's market. So I get off my bike and walk it through the pedestrian-filled street. Finally, I see a sign for Rouffignac and I turn right. The narrow road winds through a forest. There's not a car or house in sight.

I'm in the middle of nowhere, and so I find it strange when a jogger appears. I stop my bike to ask for help.

"Excusez-moi. Rouffignac? C'est là?" I point in the direction I'm heading.

"Oui," he answers without stopping.

I continue onward. When I finally exit the scenic byway, I realize I did take the wrong road. I'm about five miles away from the mapped route. My choice: I can either take the shortcut to Rouffignac, or I can ride an extra five miles to join the planned route. I opt to take the long way.

Story of my life. While others seem content to take the easier journey, I tackle self-imposed challenges. I like this aspect of myself in many ways. It's been my reason for being, a source of recognition from others, and the surest way to feel a sense of purpose in life.

Yet, continually challenging myself feels overwhelming at times. I cram in workouts instead of carving out time for rest. I take on new projects instead of hanging out with friends. Eventually, I become tired, crabby, and exhausted from all of the striving. It's not that I want to give up my drive, because this quality serves me well. I just need to find the middle ground between action and reflection.

Today, our route takes us through cave country. (In France, caves are called *grottes*.) In Montignac I plan on touring a replica of the Grotte de Lascaux, the famous cave with 17,000-year-old drawings and paintings.

The prehistoric cave was unearthed in September 1940 by four teenage boys romping in the woods. According to one version of the story, one of the boys had a dog that chased a rabbit into a hole. While climbing down to rescue the dog, the boys slid and tumbled their way into a large cave. They discovered ancient preserved art depicting large red cows, yellow horses, bulls, and stags which leapt across the cave walls. The boys were in awe, as was the world upon hearing of the remarkable find. Lascaux became known as "the prehistoric Sistine Chapel" and up to 1,700 people a day clamored to see the cave when it was opened to the public after World War II.

All of those visitors spoiled the beauty they had only intended to admire. Their shoes brought in micro-organisms which caused algae to grow on the cave floors. Their breath expelled carbon dioxide and water vapor, forming an acidic vapor that corroded the rock face and eroded pigments from the cave paintings. By 1963, the French government had no choice: the cave had to be closed to preserve its splendor. Twenty years later, the government created a replica of the cave for tourists.

Admittedly, touring a faux cave doesn't thrill like seeing the real thing, but sometimes, a facsimile is better than nothing at all. (Clarification: This is *not* true in dating.) I decide to tour the recreated cave, but first, my stomach reminds me it's lunchtime.

I stop at a grocer for fruit and a Coca Light (as they call Diet Coke here). Then I find a *boulangerie* and buy a *pain au chocolat*. This heavenly treat has become an addiction for me. The saltiness of the croissant in contrast with the sweetness of the chocolate chunks enchants my taste buds. While I normally wouldn't indulge daily in a sweet treat, I think, *Why not?* I'm burning a zillion calories a day, and back home, my pastry choices are massive muffins and dense donuts.

Do I love the *pain au chocolat* for the flavor or for the fond memories? Although my last interaction with Dante ended badly, with me calling him a jackass, we shared many wonderful moments together, like the time I visited him in Montreal.

We had been seeing each other for three months when he bought me a ticket to visit him on the East Coast. He worked in Vermont, and during the spring and summer he spent time in Montreal, where he had an apartment. I felt really hopeful with his invitation; it seemed like our relationship could *really* go somewhere.

While spending our first night in Montreal, I kept waking up, which is typical of my insomniac nature. "Go back to sleep," Dante said the first time I awoke. "It's only two in the morning in Montana."

Every time I stirred, his gentle assurances repeatedly eased me back to sleep. Finally at ten, he nudged me awake. I couldn't believe that I had slept so late.

"Wake up, sleepy. I have some breakfast for you." I was surprised to see him dressed and holding paper cups in a carrier while he put a plate on the nightstand beside the bed.

"I wasn't sure if you'd want coffee or tea, so I brought both," he said.

"Coffee would be great." I shifted the pillow to prop myself into a sitting position.

He handed me a *café au lait* and a plate with a pastry on it.

"What's this?" I asked, pointing to the pastry.

"It's *pain au chocolat.* Try it. You'll love it."

"Mmmm. This is so good. Thank you. I can't remember the last time I had breakfast in bed."

"My pleasure, *madame.*"

The memories of my Montreal morning drift away, and I return to the present and feel the sun's warmth on my shoulders. Relationships are complicated and sometimes not logical. I had been so mad at Dante before I left, but the truth is that I still care. I sit on the curb as I finish the *pain au chocolat* and the rest of my lunch watching the tourists scurry by. I'm in no rush, content to soak in the scene.

On my way to Montignac I passed Keith and Jenny, who had stopped to change a flat. I spot them now as they arrive. Keith is my age, while Jenny, his girlfriend, is nearly twenty years younger. My impression from observing them at camp is that she tries hard to interest him. She told me that she was never into cycling, but Keith's family owns a bike shop. Jokingly, she said that neither Keith nor his family could accept his dating someone who didn't ride. So Jenny took up cycling. (Why are women always the ones who adapt to fit into a relationship?) Unlike Kate, she's lean and fit and seems to enjoy riding. Every day I notice that she pushes herself to ride faster and longer. I'm impressed with her progress as a cyclist.

They walk their bikes over near the curb where I'm sitting.

"Hi. You two going to see the cave?"

"Hopefully. The line looks long," says Keith in his northern English accent.

They lock their bikes and wait in line. It never occurred to me to bring a lock to France. Since I don't have one, I'm reluctant to leave my bicycle unattended while I visit the cave. Looking around, I notice tourists with cameras dangling from their necks and kids by their sides. I doubt that any of these people would throw down their cameras, abandon their families, and pedal away on my bicycle— especially without cleated shoes. Still, to be safe, I stash my bike in a nook away from the tourists and wait in line. After fifteen minutes, the ticket line hasn't budged. I skip the cave, say goodbye to Keith and Jenny, and head to Sarlat, our destination for the night.

The route to Sarlat passes caves and remnants of prehistoric and early settlements. Halfway between Montignac and Les Eyzies is the Roque Saint-Christophe. The natural hollows of this imposing cliff were occupied by ancient people more than 55,000 years ago. Then, in the Middle Ages, the Roque Saint-Christophe became a city that lasted until the Renaissance. As I ride by, I imagine what the houses built into the cliff would look like inside. How did the cave dwellers sleep on their rock-hard floors? Did these ancient people become accustomed to it, just like I'm getting used to sleeping on the thin sleeping pad in my tent?

Farther down the road, I see a goose farm. Our tour notes say that this area of France is known for *foie gras*, goose or duck liver pâté. The birds stare at me behind a wire mesh fence, happily ignorant to their fate as fine French cuisine. I pull over to take pictures of the geese, and a woman stops her car to join me in taking photos.

"Poor things! They have no idea what they're in for," the woman says in English with an American accent. And not just any old American accent: she sounds like she's from Minnesota. Judy is only the third American I've seen since arriving.

Wait. How did she know I could speak English? Do I radiate my American-ness? Is there a homing signal between U.S. citizens? I skip these questions, and instead I ask Judy where she's from. Just as I thought: she's a Minnesotan. Like me. Although I grew up and now live in Montana, I was born in Minnesota and went to college there, so I claim both as my home states. Judy has visited Spain and Portugal, and now she's traveling alone in France. Like me. Judy claims she has enjoyed her adventure, but I have the impression she would have preferred a partner to join in her fun. Like me.

For the first time, I feel lonely in France.

Alone. Alone. Alone. Life isn't supposed to be this way. Hey, I'm not perfect; my mere presence isn't going to stop traffic. Still, I should have someone to share my vacations. Hell, I should have someone in my life. I never intended to be single for so many years after my divorce. It didn't seem so bad when Alex lived at home, but once she left for college, life felt empty without her—without someone. Now the busyness fills my time, but not the ache of loneliness. I know I can't dwell in self-pity; it's not my style. So I do what I've always done: move on and out of the way of despair. I get back on my bike.

My legs seem heavy as I start riding. I have some hills to tackle, and I'm worried about my climbing stamina. Am I tired from four long days of riding? Did I not eat enough for lunch? Or could my pity party have sapped my strength? Maybe all of these factors have worn me down. To make it worse, my right knee aches, and I'm getting saddle sore. I forgot to pack chamois cream, fondly known as butt butter, which can prevent chafing from happening in the first place. Now I'm paying the price.

I continue on and this time avoid the long way, a scenic route that travels by the castles of Beynac and Castelnaud, which face each other across the Dordogne. Our tour notes say it would be criminal to miss the spectacular Beynac castle. I don't care. I'm worn out and take the shortcut, the highway to Sarlat. With cars zipping past, a hill to climb, and a brisk wind, the ride tests my will. I grit out the final eight miles, which seem like fifty. At last I see houses on the hillside indicating I've reached Sarlat. On top of the hill is a roadside shrine, and I thank God I've made it. I've never been so happy to be done with a ride.

Sarlat is a larger city than many I have passed through. It includes a medieval section, which looks like it would have in the fourteenth century. The narrow streets are now pathways for a pedestrian mall.

The cobblestone road sends shock waves through my bike as I pass over the rock. My aching bottom radiates pain. I ride slowly, looking for a bar that will have the Tour de France on television and serve food. I find an uncrowded place and start to bring my bicycle into the bar. The waitress rushes to the door to greet me.

"Non. Laissez le vélo dehors."

This isn't a welcoming reception. She's telling me to leave my bike outside. But hey, I understand! My French comprehension is definitely improving, even after a few days. Still, I don't have a lock and this place looks even busier than Montignac. I can definitely envision the young men loitering outside stealing my bike. How can I sit inside the bar and watch my bike outside? The waitress points across the street.

I walk my bike over the cobblestone to where she has indicated. While I may not have a traveling companion, I've become attached to my two-wheeled escort. I set him against a brick wall and notice how sleek and attractive he looks leaning there. Though he's mute, he seems to call out: *Don't leave me.* I'm reluctant to walk away.

My affection for my bike reminds me of a television documentary I once saw featuring a woman enamored with the Eiffel Tower. Her love proved so boundless that she decided to marry it. Yes, *the* Eiffel Tower. She changed her name to Erika La Tour Eiffel (the French name for her big guy). Now I assume Erika and her tall, strong husband enjoyed a honeymoon, but I don't remember Erika revealing sexual details. Makes me wonder: how would she know which part was which?

People like her who have sexual feelings for inanimate objects are called *objectum-sexuals*. Let me be clear: I have no plans to marry—or sleep with—my bicycle. I'm not changing my name to Nancy La Bicyclette. Still, I have formed a bond with my handsome friend. He's more reliable than most men I've dated. They all seem dependable when you first start dating, but then little cracks form on their shiny exteriors. At first Jeff wanted to include me on all of his bike rides. Then after a few months, he told me that I wasn't fast enough to ride with his friends, and he wanted to cycle without me. Jim claimed I was the love of his life until he found someone who lived closer to him and married her instead. I think dealing with rejection never gets easier.

I leave my bike and return to the bar. Relaxing on a stool, I order a ham and cheese sandwich with a glass of red wine. The sandwich is massive and served on a whole baguette. It's more than a foot long—a true *Grand Derrière* Baguette—with mounds of thinly-sliced ham piled with white cheese. As always in France, the bread is served dry without even a thin spread of butter. (And, by the way, the only sandwiches the French seem to serve are ham, cheese, or ham and cheese.) I doubt I can eat the whole thing, but I open my mouth wide and take my first bite. Five minutes later, I've devoured the entire humongous sandwich.

Maybe I need more food to avoid losing energy during my rides. Nate has been nagging me to eat more. Maybe he's right: I am burning an extra 2,500 calories or more every day. For now, my belly is full. I relax at the bar sipping my wine as I watch the time trial of the Tour de France, all the while eyeing my bike. I need to find a lock.

After my break, I ride up a steep hill toward my campground, which is not easy to find. I stop midway when I see the second random man of the day. This one is walking down the road, not jogging. I ask for help once again, and he confirms that I'm headed toward my campground. I try to start pedaling, but the hill is steep where I've stopped, and my legs are so tired that I can't. I walk my bike on my cleated shoes for a few hundred feet until the road flattens, and then I start again.

I enter the campground, not sure if I am in the right place. Then I see some of the cycling group. I need to set up my tent, but first I'll have afternoon tea—truly a misnomer. I pile my plate with snacks, pour a glass of wine, and gracelessly plop down on one of the plastic chairs. All dignity dissipates when the exhaustion of a ride kicks in.

"Did you have a tough day of riding?" asks Ian, who is also sitting under the canopy.

"I'm exhausted."

"You should try some Vegemite. That will perk you up."

"What's that?" He shows me a bright yellow jar.

"Here, try it," he says, spreading some of the brown paste within the jar onto a piece of bread. I take a bite, and it tastes like yeasty paste. I spit it out.

"Ehhh. That's awful!"

"It's very good for you—lots of vitamin B."

Apparently Vegemite has iconic popularity in Australia. It's a dark brown food paste made of yeast extract. I suppose it's an acquired taste, like lutefisk, which is popular in Minnesota, but I don't plan on eating that either. It's so horrible that I wish I had mouthwash. I don't, so I wash away the taste with a gulp of wine.

Tonight, I expected to sleep well. I don't, but for once, it isn't the campground sounds that cause insomnia. It's the thoughts of Dante that keep me awake.

U.S. DATING FACTS

- **95.9 million** – Number of unmarried Americans eighteen and older in 2008. This group comprised 43 percent of all U.S. residents eighteen and older. (U.S. Census)

- **34** – Percent of women over forty who are "cougars"—or dating younger men. (AARP survey)

- **87** – Number of unmarried men eighteen and older for every 100 unmarried women in the United States. (U.S. Census)

- **68** – Percent of forty-plus women who haven't been on a date in the past three years and say they just aren't interested in dating or being in a romantic relationship. (AARP)

- **51** – Percent of unmarried women in the U.S. (U.S. Census)

- **More than 20 million** – Number of people who visit at least one online dating service a month. (Online Dating Magazine)

- **6 million** – Number of dates that Match.com members go on each year. (Match.com)

- **28** – Percent of single people in New York City, the "Best City for Singles" (Forbes)

- **63** – Percent of single women living alone who say their older years are the time to pursue their dreams. (AARP)

Chapter 11

BLIND DATE

Meeting Dante started with a cryptic voicemail last February.

"Hey, Nancy, this is Charles. I want to set you up on a blind date but not with a blind guy. He's a friend of mine, a doc-tore. Call me."

Lovable, quirky Charles. The guy would do anything for one of his friends, but other times, you'd wonder why you *were* his friend. He reminded me of George Costanza, Jerry's exasperating pal on Seinfeld. He not only resembled George, but he was always stirring things up like Jerry's sidekick. But his heart was good, even though he sometimes frustrated me.

Charles and I met through Toastmasters more than ten years ago. We became better friends when we enrolled together in Coach Jay's wind-training class. He played cupid then as well when he set me up with Jeff.

Knowing Charles, I wasn't surprised with his cryptic message about the blind date. My expectations were low, and I didn't call that night. I wasn't *that* desperate.

I waited until the morning when I saw Charles at Toastmasters. I approached him after the meeting.

"So tell me about this guy that you want to set me up with."

"He's a doc-tore. What more do you need to know?" Charles acted nonchalant, putting on his jacket.

"Plenty. How old is he?"

"Our age." He put his hands in his jacket pockets, sensing my barrage of questions.

"Is he a young-looking forty-something or old-looking?"

Charles paused for a moment. "He looks good."

"Is he a short dude?" That would have been a huge issue for me.

"No, he's about this tall." Charles, who stands about five-foot-eight, demonstrated the doc-tore's height by raising his hand five inches over his head.

My most important question was next.

"Does he bike?" Charles was a competitive cyclist, and so he knew what I meant by this. I didn't want some wannabe biker who didn't even own riding shorts.

"Yeah, he bikes." Charles took his hands out of his pockets and crossed them in front of him. I think he was getting weary of my questions.

"Can he keep up with me?"

"He bikes well. You'll like him."

I was still skeptical, but I agreed to meet the doc-tore, a.k.a. Dante.

By Friday, Charles called with Dante's Web site where I could find his contact information. I checked out the site, found his last name, and did a search on the physician directory to track down his picture. He looked date-worthy—dark hair, nice smile, stylish glasses.

I felt awkward calling, so I emailed Dante saying I was a friend of Charles. His return email made me laugh. He told me it must have been "scary beyond words" to admit that I was a friend of Charles. After a few emails, he asked me out for Valentine's Day. We agreed to meet at nine at a local bar for pizza—after Coach Jay's wind-training class. (Hey, I had my priorities!)

I walked in looking for the black and red cycling jacket that he had said he would be wearing, but I couldn't see him. Then he noticed me and waved me over to the bar. I was surprised. His photo didn't convey his handsome face and lean biking physique. How could this good-looking man be waiting for me?

I sat next to Dante at the bar, and he warmly greeted me. He asked if I wanted a drink. I declined. He ordered a glass of water for me, a microbrew for himself, and a large pepperoni pizza for us to share. Charles was the perfect icebreaker for our conversation. Then we talked about work and cycling. I liked his biking stories. I liked the way he looked. I liked his sense of humor. I could *really* fall for this guy.

The bar stool next to me was empty, and a man in his mid-twenties with a baseball cap sat down.

"Do you want some candy?" he asked as he showed me a bowl full of taffy.

"Sure," I said and took a piece of candy. He reached across me and showed the bowl to Dante, who also took some.

I should have learned in my youth to never take candy from a stranger. The sweets were bait to initiate conversation. The man on the barstool, Ryan, wouldn't shut up. He worked at the bar as a cook, he had made our pizza, and now he was off work. Ryan started off normally enough by telling us his secret to making really good pizzas. Then the conversation turned personal as Ryan explained that he had recently moved out of the place he shared with his girlfriend and child. He was living with his parents, which wasn't working out too well.

"My mom won't leave me alone. Always nagging me to make my bed and pick up my clothes. I like to leave my clothes right where I take them off. Why should she care? And then she has me wash my clothes every three days—even if I don't have a full load. It's nuts!"

He was nuts. He was also becoming drunk, slamming down six drinks in an hour. This was moderation, Ryan claimed. He now stopped his nightly binge at least eight hours before his next work shift. In addition to his relationship, home, and drinking problems, Ryan had a gambling addiction. He tried to stay away from casinos.

Why was this random guy telling me all of his personal business? I wanted it to stop. I'm not a meek person, and normally I'd have no problem telling someone like Ryan to get lost. Yet, I was on a first date with someone I liked, and I wanted to make a good impression. The bar was loud, and Dante couldn't hear most of the nonsense. Lucky him. He sat quietly, eating pizza and sipping his beer. He didn't seem bothered.

At ten thirty, Dante asked if I was ready to go. I felt disappointed. After a great start with Dante, my Valentine's dinner had ended as a date from hell with Ryan.

"The two of you seemed to hit it off," Dante said as we left the bar.

"Are you kidding? I was ready to kill myself. I should have said something to him."

"Good thing you didn't. He makes good pizzas. I'd hate to have him mad and make a bad one next time." I saw a hint of a smile cross his face. He was teasing me.

We walked to the end of the block and stopped at the curb, waiting for a car before we crossed the street.

"I had fun tonight," I said. "I just wish we could have talked more."

"We can still talk. I live just across the street. Do you want to come up for a glass of wine?"

Maybe our date would have a better ending after all. We walked up the rickety stairs to his apartment. His place was sparsely furnished: a tall round table with two chairs, a bed, two nightstands, and a table with a TV. I was surprised by his humble living situation, considering he was a doctor. In his living room, where a couch would be expected, were two bikes. One was a road bike; the other was a 1902 replica bike with thirty-six-inch wheels. Dante demonstrated that the bike had colored lights on the spokes that spelled out "Merry Christmas" when the wheels turned. The guy was a bit quirky.

He poured us each a glass of wine and gave me the one real wine glass he owned. As we sat down at his table to sip wine, Dante talked about his work and how he split his time between Montana and Vermont.

"How does that work?" I was curious how someone could live two places as a doctor.

"I help out for vacation coverage. I set up my schedule for a year at a time for each place," he said. "Sometimes I can be here a month or two at a time. Other times, I'll be gone to Vermont for that long."

"When are you going back?" I asked. He really seemed like someone I would like to get to know better.

"I'm leaving Saturday."

I felt disappointed. So much promise, and he was leaving in four days.

"We really live different lives," I said. My two dogs, banking job, and houseful of belongings wouldn't accommodate this vagabond lifestyle. I didn't know at the time that my words would haunt me over the coming months.

Dante and I talked until midnight, which was surprising, considering I'm not a night owl and had to work the next day. The conversation flowed, the wine went down easily, and Dante captivated me. He walked me outside to my car, and I thought about the kiss—I wanted one, but nothing too passionate.

His response was perfect—a half hug and a quick peck on the lips. I drove away with a smile on my face. Thanks, Charles.

Chapter 12

Au Revoir, MONTREAL

Since our first date on Valentine's Day, I had seen Dante each time he returned to Montana. And now it was May, and I was traveling to the East Coast to spend a week with him in his other world.

I flew into JFK Airport in New York on Sunday, and he rode his bike more than 300 miles from Vermont to meet me. We stayed in a suite at a boutique hotel in Manhattan. The next day we walked through the city. He casually relaxed his arm around my shoulders as we strolled through Manhattan. I loved feeling like part of a couple.

My favorite destination was a restaurant near the Brooklyn promenade where we sat outside sharing a bottle of red wine and a basket of sesame seed bread while we watched the colorful people walk by. We made up stories for each person. The guy with the too-tight suit worked as a vacuum salesperson. The woman with the high heels and big hair was rushing home to primp for her married lover.

After a night in New York, we rode the Amtrak to Vermont and explored the state by car and bike. On Friday, we were on our way to Montreal to spend the weekend at his apartment.

"Drive faster," said Dante.

"I don't want a ticket," I said. "The speed limit is 100. I'm at 110."

"You won't get a ticket."

"Well, I don't want to take a chance in a foreign country."

"Come on. We're going to be late."

I pressed my foot on the accelerator, letting the speed reach 115 kilometers per hour. I clenched the steering wheel, trying to bury my frustration.

"What kind of bike race starts at ten at night anyway?"

"It's a fun race."

"Sure, for you. You didn't ride forty miles today." I had ridden that morning while Dante worked.

"You'll do fine."

"I don't even have aerobars. How am I supposed to ride fast?"

"Don't worry so much."

In a time-trial race, it would be just me against the clock. Successful racers maintain a crouched position to cut wind resistance, which can be achieved with a special time-trial bicycle or aerobars. I had no chance of doing well without the right equipment.

We drove in silence the rest of the way to his Montreal apartment. It was after ten and dark outside as we pulled up.

"Looks like we missed the race," I said. "We can still make it if we hurry," he answered.

I didn't want to race when I couldn't ride well. Why did we have to rush to a bike race anyway? But I didn't want to complain and spoil the great week we had shared. I kept quiet.

We rode the elevator to the fourteenth floor of Dante's building and walked down the hall to his apartment. There was no time for a tour, he told me. He brought his bag into the bedroom. I set my large suitcase on the living room floor and crouched beside it. I lifted piles of clothes and stacked them on the carpet, trying to piece together a cycling outfit. Within minutes, Dante emerged dressed and ready to bike. I hadn't even found everything I would need to wear, much less put it on.

"Come on. We need to go or we'll miss the race," he said.

"Look. I'm doing the best I can. It's raining outside, and I can't even find my fucking arm warmers."

He paused. "You don't have to go if you don't want to."

"I'm going." I grabbed my jacket from the bottom of one of the piles on the floor, tipping the clothes on top into a messy mound. I stomped into his bedroom to dress. When I returned to the living room, Dante asked a question.

"What bikes should we take?" I saw a bit of amusement in his eyes as he said this.

"What do you mean?" I asked.

"Should we take the road bikes or these?" he said, pointing to the two 1902 replicas.

Oh God, he had only been joking when he said it was a time-trial race. It couldn't be a race if we were riding the replicas. And I had been so bitchy.

"Let's take the big bikes," I said, smiling sheepishly.

"Come on. Let's hurry." He gave me a quick kiss.

We rode to the start of the Tour la Nuit (Tour the Night in English), a nighttime cycling adventure through the streets of Montreal. It didn't matter that we were late. With more than ten thousand other riders, we soon caught up to the back of the pack. The ride was more like a parade than a race. Cyclists glowed from colored lights attached to helmets, wheels, and everywhere between. They rode all kinds of bicycles, from high-end road bikes to handmade concoctions assembled in their garages.

The riders alongside me found me intriguing. Actually, they liked the bike. Not only were the thirty-six-inch wheels a conversation piece, but so were the Hokey Spokes, bright neon lights that created patterns as my wheels turned.

"Ha, ha, ha! Le blah, le blah, le blah." They'd point, laugh and utter words in their Montreal-accented French. I had no idea what they were saying. Dante had spent a lot of time in Montreal, so he understood and would answer, sometimes translating for me. I didn't want to talk anyway. I was enjoying the experience of riding through the night on this big-ass bike as spectators standing in the drizzle shouted:

"Allez! Allez! Allez!"

I loved our first bike ride in Montreal. The second ride the next day wasn't as much fun.

"Do you have a spare?" I asked Dante before we even left his apartment.

"Yes, right here," he answered, grabbing a plastic baggie, which he put in his back jersey pocket.

Leaving the big bikes at home, we jumped on our road bikes and headed toward the suburbs. Twenty miles into the ride, Dante's bike tire deflated. We stopped, and he pulled the baggie out of his back jersey pocket. No inner tube. He had also forgotten his cell phone. No taxi.

We were stranded in the middle of a suburban neighborhood in the early evening. We saw neither stores nor people.

"I remember a bike shop down the road," I said. "Maybe we can get a tube there."

We spun our bikes around and walked toward the city. Imagine walking with a lump in the middle of your foot; that's what it's like to walk on cleats. Our shoes clicked slowly down the street. Then Dante had an idea.

"Let's ride on your bike together."

"How can we do that?"

"I'll be in front and pedal. You can sit and hold onto my bike."

What a ludicrous idea, but oh, well.

"OK. Let's try," I said.

I straddled the bike.

"Now hold my bike."

"Where?"

"Hold the seat."

Dante lifted his leg over the top tube and stood in front of me.

"Now I'll hold the bike steady, and you sit down."

"OK, I'm on. Where should I put my feet?"

"Just put them behind you."

Dante stood and pedaled. We moved slowly, but riding was faster than walking on cleats.

"Hang on," I said. "I'm losing my grip on your bike."

He stopped. I repositioned my hand on his bike saddle.

"OK. Ready."

He started again. I could hear him huffing and puffing. I noticed a car drive by and the people crane their necks to check us out as they passed.

"Did you see that?"

"What?"

"The people!"

We obviously looked ridiculous—two adults on a bike with another bike rolling beside. I started to laugh—so hard that I began to drool.

"Stop laughing!" Dante said in between ragged breaths. Still I could hear humor in his voice.

"I can't!"

"I've got to stop," he said, a bit breathless.

We stopped, I composed myself, and we started again. After a mile, we resumed walking. We made it to the bike shop. Closed.

"Now what?" I asked.

"We'll just have to keep walking."

A man on a mountain bike neared us.

"Let's ask him for help," I said. "Maybe he has a spare."

Dante flagged him down. The man spoke in French, and I didn't understand. Dante translated. The man didn't have a tube to fit the narrow road bicycle tires. Dusk was descending, and the drizzle had returned.

"This really sucks," I said. "I'm starting to get cold."

"Let's keep walking. We can catch the subway a few miles down the road."

Dante walked ahead, and I shuffled behind.

"*Salut,*" I heard from behind me.

I turned around and saw the man on the mountain bike. He spoke in French again.

"What's he saying?"

"He remembered he had a patch kit. So he thought he'd come back to help."

Dante took the wheel off his bike, then removed the tube. The man identified the puncture location in Dante's tube and patched up the hole.

So everything turned out fine, as it always seemed to when Dante forgot something. His secret? Like a Boy Scout, he was constantly prepared. Earlier in the day, he had locked his apartment keys inside his apartment. No worries. He had hidden spares outside the building. His wallet, computer, keys, credit card, and cell phone all had labels with his name, phone number, and the word "Reward." I was surprised that Dante didn't have spare tubes stashed throughout the city.

He was absentminded, yet I found his idiosyncrasies charming. More than charming, he was also fun, adventurous, and doting. I could tell that I had fallen in love with him. But I didn't really know how he felt. Did he think he could have a future with me? I found out the following day.

Our final ride in Montreal came the next morning. We waited along with 30,000 citizen riders for the start of our last ride through the city. We would cycle fifty kilometers (about thirty-one miles) around the island in the Tour de l'Île (Tour of the Island). The cold, overcast day matched my somber mood. Dante noticed.

"Kiss me," he said.

"I don't want to." I stood beside him, but I didn't even look his way when I answered.

"Smile," Dante said as he attempted to lift the corners of my mouth with his fingers.

I didn't want to kiss him. I didn't want to smile. My mouth drooped to a frown. As we stood near the starting line, Dante took my picture on his cell phone. My face displayed my gloom. I gave him a half smile as I realized how terrible I must look. He retook the picture.

"Let's talk after the ride," he said.

I told him OK and kissed him quickly despite my sadness.

What a terrible ending to a magical week. Dante had thrown a cold glass of water on my hopes as we lay in bed on our last morning together. I had asked him whether he could see a future between us. Without hesitation, he had said no; a relationship was out of the question. "You said it yourself. We have too many life differences. I've traveled and experienced things that you haven't."

How could I have responded? My answer had been silence, my habit when he made blunt proclamations during an otherwise intimate time. Every time we had seemed to get close, he had pushed me away. This hadn't been the first time he had brought up our differences.

I wanted a relationship. He wanted no commitments. I liked having my roots in one place. He liked living in multiple cities. I had a daughter, two dogs, a cat, and a goldfish. He had his solitude and precious freedom.

As I waited at the starting line I reflected on our week together. A part of me felt ridiculous for falling for his obviously contrived charm. Another part of me didn't believe he could really fake having so much fun. I've always heard that you can tell a lot by a person's actions and should trust those over words. But what if the actions contradicted the words? How could someone radiate the warmth of sunshine and say words that stung like an arctic front?

He had accused me of using our Montreal trip to explore our "coupledom" when all he had wanted was someone familiar to show his life to back east. It hadn't mattered that it was me—anyone he knew would have been fine. Then why hadn't he bought Charles a ticket instead?

But he had picked me. While Dante showed me his outer world on the East Coast, I had begun revealing my inner world of vulnerability. I had let down my guard and allowed myself to feel love for him. Yes, it had been a cautious, guarded love that I hadn't expressed out loud, not at that point anyway. As my soft side surfaced, his cool remarks had struck my very core.

We rode the Tour de l'Île at a slow pace, despite taking our road bikes. Not that our goal was speeding through the streets of Montreal, but some of the riders dawdled. Kids pedaled pastel two-wheelers. Parents pulled children in carts behind their bicycles. Novice riders had dusted the cobwebs off their vintage bikes for the first time in years. All came out to ride through the streets of Montreal on a cold and windy day. These Montrealers were hearty people.

Our ride concluded just as the rain started. We escaped the drizzle by stopping at a café where we ordered *crêpes chocolat* and coffee.

We needed to talk, but I feared bringing up what troubled me most: Dante didn't want a relationship with me. I let him ramble on about our life differences and what he meant by his earlier comments. He said that he wasn't trying to be arrogant or indicate that he was better than me because of his travels, education, and worldliness as compared to my life as a single parent in suburban Montana. Yet, wasn't that exactly what he was doing in pointing out our differences?

The breakfast eased the hunger, and the conversation pacified the tension between us, even though we resolved nothing. We returned to his apartment. I showered, dressed, and packed while he meticulously cleaned the bikes. He drove me to the airport.

"Just drop me off."

"I'm going in."

I gave him five Canadian dollars to cover his parking. Dante had misplaced his wallet, which didn't surprise me. Someone would call about it eventually.

We went inside the airport, and I checked in. Then we stopped at the bar to order drinks. I bought. We talked and drank longer than his money would stretch to cover parking, so I gave him another five bucks.

Dante walked me to the security check-in. He gave me two French cheek kisses goodbye, and I turned away and started walking toward customs clearance.

"Nancy, do you want me to wait?"

Yes, I wanted to say. *I want you to wait for me forever.* Instead, I turned around and retraced my steps. A velvet rope divided us.

"Do you want me to wait? Make sure your plane leaves on time?"

I didn't answer. My arms reached out to him, and I gave him a warm embrace and adoring kiss goodbye. He returned the kiss with equal affection.

"Call me if you get delayed. I'll come back and get you."

At that moment I forgot his icy words from earlier in the day and didn't care if I ever left Montreal. I wanted to pretend our conversation hadn't happened, and lose myself in our magical world from earlier in the week.

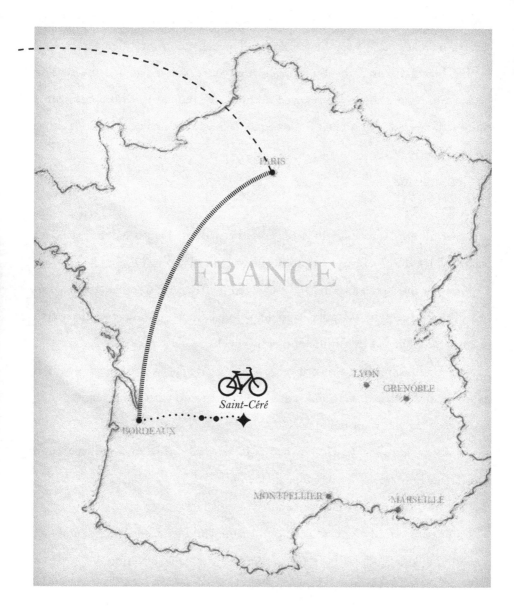

ROUTE NOTES: *Cycle from Sarlat to Saint-Céré. Stop at Rocamadour, a medieval city built into limestone cliffs.*

DISTANCE: *60 miles or 97 kilometers*

Chapter 13

ON THE ROAD
TO ROCAMADOUR

I'm not the fastest hill climber, but today I push as I wind my way out of Sarlat. Head down, steady cadence, I pass some tour riders who left before me. I'm riding well after such a difficult time yesterday. As I near the crest, I see it all unfold before me.

A navy Saab backs out of a driveway on my left. A black Mercedes is traveling fast downhill. The downhill driver sees the Saab and slams his brakes. It's too late.

SCREECH! SLAM!

The impact pushes the cars toward me. There's nowhere to go. I must stop or ride into the ditch. As I start braking, I struggle to unclip my left foot, but my shoe won't release. The cars barrel closer. I twist harder, and my shoe unclips. I clutch my brakes tightly and come to a stop. The cars stop six feet away, both crumpled with smoke rising from their hoods. Radiator fluid pours from one vehicle. The smell of burning rubber assaults my nose.

I could have been killed.

The man who pulled out of the driveway exits his car first. His balding head bleeds from a gash. The man and woman in the Mercedes appear unhurt as they emerge from their car. The woman walks to the side of the road, sits down in the grass, and rests her head between her knees. She must be thinking *she* could have been killed.

I walk uphill and wave to an oncoming car. The driver stops and turns on hazard lights. My cycling companions are behind me. I wait for them.

"What happened?" asks Ellie.

"The guy. He pulled out in front of the other car. Right in front of me."

"Are you OK?"

"I'm fine." I'm lying, but they don't need to know. It's easier to be tough rather than welcome comfort.

Ellie suggests that everyone hoist their bikes over the debris, and we follow her lead. Once back on my bicycle, I surge ahead. I want to cry but don't. I ride hard to forget my swirling emotions. Maybe I shouldn't have taken off but allowed myself to feel the comfort of the group. This is the second time I've been saved from disaster. It's no coincidence. My guardian angel has protected me.

Yes, I do believe in guardian angels. I'm not exactly sure how it works, but I trust that unseen guides accompany us in life and look out for us. How do I know? I've never seen one. I've never heard one's voice. It's a sense, an instinct. Sometimes in my life, I literally feel guided by an unseen force. Now, it's always my choice what I will do with the guidance. I can disregard the advice I'm sensing, but I've learned through the years that it's best to listen.

I remember reading in the book *Eat, Pray, Love* that Elizabeth Gilbert wrote to God in the midst of divorcing her husband. She petitioned God to help end the conflict and bitterness between them so they could amicably part. Instantly after she wrote the petition, her lawyer called to let her know that her husband had agreed to the divorce.

Gilbert had her doubts about writing to God, and it's a stretch for me as well. Doesn't God have more important things to do than responding to my trivia? I think it would be like asking the Queen of England for help. I doubt she would have time to reply either. But I can imagine that someone who works for the Queen would send me a response, just as I think that someone who works for God could give me guidance.

So like Elizabeth Gilbert, I ask for guidance—not from God, but from my angels. I write my questions to the angels, and the answers form messages in my mind. I feel like a scribe, putting the words down on paper. Or sometimes I'll awake with an insightful breakthrough idea related to my concern.

Now I will confess: the answers aren't always what I desire. For example, if I write to ask how I can attract a certain man back into my life, invariably the angels tell me that I need to focus on *my* life and how to make it better. The longing represents a missing piece within me. Thanks a lot, angels. They're right, of course, but it's not what I want to hear.

I've found my angels particularly vigilant while I'm traveling. Once about ten years ago, I ran my car off the road in a blizzard while riding through a desolate section of eastern Montana. My daughter, who was around twelve at the time, panicked.

"Oh, no! Mom! How are we going to get out of here? We're going to be stuck in the cold!"

"Don't worry. The angels will take care of us. You'll see."

Just as the words escaped my lips, not one but six strapping men dressed in Carhartt jackets and overalls materialized from every direction and ran toward my car. One carried a shovel over his shoulders. The handsome men heaved my car out of the snow bank and back onto the road. We didn't even step out of the car. Alex's mouth gaped open as she watched the scene. We both burst out in laughter as we headed down the road. She still talks about it.

I have many more examples of my road angels at work, but the details aren't important. I just know that angels are watching out for me.

I'm on my own once again, riding hard, and the challenging pace keeps my mind off the accident. There's little traffic on this road. It's just me, my bike, and the beauty of the Périgord Noir forest. The sunshine warms my back and illuminates the lush green foliage with an iridescent glow.

I pass a woman on a bicycle with a young girl pedaling behind her on a tandem bike. Riding ahead, I stop and ask if I can take their photo. The woman also stops, and we talk in English. She's Dutch and knows several languages. That's one thing that surprises me. In France, many people—even the campground staff—are multilingual. The woman introduces herself as Josie. She shares that she and her family moved from the Netherlands to France due to her husband's work. I take their photo and show Josie the digital image through the viewfinder.

Josie's little girl is dressed in a flowered shirt and matching fuchsia helmet. She reminds me of my own blonde darling, now a grown-up college student living more than 1,600 miles from home. Alex's first two emails haven't alleviated my concerns of leaving her to manage the house on her own.

"Last night I almost started the house on fire!" (Does the exclamation point mean emergency or excitement?) "We were lighting fireworks and one that shoots exploding balls of fire in the air tipped toward the house and started firing red flames at us. I felt like I was in a war zone!"

According to Alex, our neighbor watched the whole incident and told her that her display was more entertaining than the city's fireworks.

In her next email she talked about Zimmer, my heeler/husky mutt, making his escape. "Goodness, I am *soooo* sick of him running away from home."

Alex *is* my family. I'll admit she lifted my spirits during the trying times following my divorce when I lost my husband, business, and house all within a year. I needed a purpose and a focus; she needed my attention and guidance. At twenty, she still needs some advice from time to time, but she has grown into an independent and self-directed young lady.

After riding thirty miles, I arrive atop the cliffs above Rocamadour. Travel guides have told me that Rocamadour is the second most popular tourist site in France, after Mont Saint-Michel in Normandy. (They must not be counting Paris.) Tourist numbers do nothing to prepare me for the beauty that awaits me. From my vantage point, I can see the magical village below built into the face of a 500-foot limestone cliff. How can a city from centuries ago be constructed in such a manner? It's astonishing.

I start my exploration at a prehistoric cave located atop the cliff. Unlike Montignac, this cave has no long ticket line, and I pay my entrance fee without delay. Before I go inside, I secure my bike with a lock I bought before I left Sarlat.

The tour guide speaks French, but I'm provided notes in English. They are of little use in a dark cave. I strain to understand her French words and to see the cave walls, which the tour guide lights up with brief strobes of a flashlight. She explains the cave includes ancient pictographs—estimated at 20,000 years old. There are pictures of horses and an elk, plus hand prints. Since I can't understand most of her lecture, I let my imagination fill in the blanks. I speculate that the art must have been the work of some bored prehistoric teenager.

"Oh for goodness' sake, Humphrey," his mom must have scolded, "why don't you just entertain yourself by working on an art project?"

Embedded in the cave rock are a fossilized fish jaw and a plant, which looks like a piece of wheat sticking out of the ceiling. The cave must have been underwater before Humphrey's family lived there.

More recent history lies across the street at the Shrine of Our Lady of Rocamadour, a compound of religious structures with the tomb of an ancient saint. As the legend goes, a Christian hermit, Saint Amadour, witnessed the martyrdom of Saint Paul and Saint Peter. It's claimed that he may have even conversed with Jesus.

Saint Amadour died around 70 AD, and more than a millennium later his grave was discovered and in it his perfectly preserved body. Claims of miracles flourished in the village and it became a popular destination for pilgrims thereafter. Today, Saint Amadour's crypt is considered an ideal place for worship and meditation.

Near the crypt stands the Chapel of Our Lady, which houses the Black Madonna—a twelfth-century statue of the Virgin Mary with baby Jesus. Many chapel visitors light candles and pray to the Blessed Virgin. And legends claim that at times Mary has even responded to prayers by ringing the bell suspended from the ceiling.

I walk inside the chapel to say a prayer of thanks for my safety. I know divine intervention allowed me to walk away from two accidents. My spirit fills with gratitude at my protection during my travels as I sit inside the peaceful sanctuary. The bell doesn't spontaneously ring, but I feel a sense of tranquility in the ancient stone church.

After leaving the chapel, my next stop is the village below. I'll have to descend the cliff to get to Rocamadour. I can climb down the more than 200 steps of the Grand Escalier (Great Staircase), take the elevator, or ride down the road.

The way of pilgrims is by staircase. As an act of penance, pilgrims would regularly climb the stairs on their knees. Some still do today. Our tour notes say that many Tour de France professionals train for the ride up Alpe d'Huez by climbing and kneeling up the steps. As part of our tour, we will climb up Alpe d'Huez and Mont Ventoux, which are some of the toughest cycling ascents in the world. Even if it might help my ride up these mountains, I'm not going to kneel up the steps. Even walking down the staircase with my cleated shoes seems problematic.

While the stairs are daunting, the elevator feels like cheating. So I ride my bike down the steep, narrow road to the city below. I step back in time as I view the medieval buildings lining the crooked street. People crowd the road, so I dismount my bike and walk it on the stone streets no wider than a bike path back home.

The day is sweltering and I'm hot and hungry. I have a protein bar in my back pocket, but I want some fruit to accompany it. Stopping by a restaurant, I see some of my cycling friends sitting at a table. I ask if I can join them. Simon just looks at me, not offering me a seat. Maybe he doesn't like me.

Robbie breaks the silence. "Sure, sit down, Nance."

I squeeze in beside Nate.

They get back to their conversation, talking and joking like good buddies, or mates as they would say. I sit quietly and eat my fruit. I know it's my fault: I decided to brush off my companions and travel on my own. Now I'm an outsider. They're still friendly to me, but we aren't friends—at least not the kind of friends they are with each other.

I don't enjoy feeling like the outcast, but I also realize that I've caused this by not extending myself to the others. While I've been riding solo, they've been getting to know each other on their rides. Yet, if I had spent time with them, I wouldn't have enjoyed exploring France on my own. Maybe I need a balance—to connect with my tour mates when I'm with them and still enjoy time by myself.

After a brief break, everyone is leaving. I return to my bike and start the steep ascent up the hill with Nate, Robbie, and Ian. While Robbie and Ian pedal at a leisurely pace, Nate is taking chances. A random driver agrees to let Nate hang onto his car up the steep hill. As usual, Nate rides without a helmet. Once we're out of town, Nate drafts closely behind a truck full of hay. I wonder what will happen to him if the truck stops suddenly or if one of hay bales falls off. Despite his risky behavior, he's a strong rider who keeps a good pace. I'm riding fast myself, but I drop behind Nate on our way to our campsite at Saint-Céré.

Crew leader Drew told me that camping is quite popular with the French. Many spend weeks at a campground for a summer vacation. They bring their own campers, trailers, or tents. At some campgrounds, they can rent furnished tents, bungalows, and even mobile homes. As with hotels, the French government issues star ratings to campgrounds. Three- and four-star campgrounds can be downright luxurious. The Saint-Céré campground has a four-star rating for good reason: the amenities include a swimming pool, playground, tennis and basketball courts, skateboard track, restaurant with TV, and Wi-Fi Internet access.

In some ways, French camping feels like pitching a tent in a city park. All campsites are groomed, lacking in a rustic feel common for U.S. campgrounds. As a touring cyclist, I appreciate the posh campground amenities. I like a daily shower. So what if I have to push a button several times to keep the water flowing? Flush toilets are an improvement over stinky porta-potties common in America. Meals and drinks on site are convenient after riding fifty miles or more.

One difference I don't like: campfires are never allowed. If you want to roast weenies or marshmallows over an open flame, you use propane. (Of course, this is all hypothetical as I haven't seen one weenie or marshmallow in France.) Another difference is the outdoor urinals common at many of the French campgrounds. The men think nothing of peeing *en plein air* (in the open air) for the world to see. I'm not squeamish with nakedness, but seriously, who wants to see a stranger peeing?

This evening our group dines at the Hotel Victor Hugo in Saint-Céré, a few blocks away from our campground. I'm starving from my long ride and sparse eating during the day. While I wait for dinner, I stuff myself with bread, which in France is always served without butter. Our meal is exquisite, real French fine dining with an array of gourmet dishes from which to choose: duck, rabbit, fish, or steak. (I'm reluctant to try the French steak, I admit, because I think it may disappoint when compared to beef from Montana.)

Tonight I make an effort to connect with my tour companions. It's easy to bond with Drew, who sits next to me and keeps my wine glass full—as well as his.

"Look at the sign," he says, pointing out the depiction of a young Victor Hugo. "It looks like little Vic has a problem."

"What do you mean?"

"A little problem with his package."

I see his point. Young Victor's tight pants reveal a tiny bulge, more like a bulgette. Drew reaches for the bottle of wine and refills my glass.

"Now, Victor looks much more dignified here," he says, pointing out a sketch of a more mature Hugo on the bottle.

Maybe it's the wine or my fatigue, but I find this hilarious. I laugh with Drew and take photos of both the sign and the bottle. It's good to connect after so many days of being on my own.

Victor Hugo wrote, "To contemplate is to look at shadows." I wonder if avoiding my shadow side has been creating pain in my relationships so that I gain awareness of myself. The shadow, according to the twentieth-century Swiss psychologist Carl Jung, is everything in us that is unconscious, repressed, undeveloped, and denied.

We cannot learn about ourselves if we do not learn about our shadow. And if we don't consciously explore our repressed parts, we will attract others in our lives who act as mirrors for us.

That must be what's happening with me. All of these men I've dated are reflecting parts of me that I don't want to face: the pieces that feel unconfident, unworthy, and unlovable. Unconsciously, I'll do anything to avoid my shadow, and so I search for a partner who can prove my inner doubts wrong. Maybe if the right man loves me enough, I can learn to love myself. But because I don't love myself, I attract men who reflect that back to me. This deepens my insecurities.

My dating merry-go-round is really an inner spin cycle. I cycle through this pattern to eliminate the pain within. I go in circles as I continue to look outside myself for salvation when the truth is that I must fill my own emotional cup.

When I debated coming to France, Kathleen had asked me, "Why don't you care enough about yourself to do this for you?" I'm glad I listened to her wisdom. Pursuing my innermost passions demonstrates self-love. When I return, I'm going to do things that make me happy as a way of life. I'll find time for cycling, writing, and taking photos. I'll visit places I've always wanted to see. I'll reach out to interesting new people to enliven my soul.

By facing my shadows, I still may not find a satisfying relationship, but maybe it won't matter so much. I'll have created a loving relationship with myself.

Young Victor Hugo looks like
Little Lord Fauntleroy.

A more dignified Victor Hugo.

FRENCH CAMPING: WHAT YOU NEED TO KNOW

- **Star ratings** – The French government ranks campgrounds with star ratings, just like it does for hotels and restaurants. One-star campgrounds are more rugged; those with four stars include many amenities, such as swimming pools, restaurants, and shower facilities.
- **Tent** – If you bring your own tent, make sure it's waterproof, not just water-resistant.
- **Comfort** – These items can make your camping experience more comfortable: pillow, sleeping pad, and flashlight.
- **Shower gear** – Bring at least two towels, a washcloth, flip flops or sandals, soap with a plastic case, and shampoo. You'll also want something to tote your personal items to the shower, such as a mesh bag.
- **Clothing** – Bring wrinkle-free fabrics that can line dry. This will prevent the frumpy look. Also, remember your swimsuit as many French campgrounds have swimming pools.

- **Laundry** – Many campgrounds will have on-site washing machines and dryers. You can buy laundry detergent at the campground or bring your own. Some campgrounds have clotheslines, and clothespins come in handy.

- **Accessories** – Bring plastic grocery bags and Ziploc bags, which have many uses. You may also want to carry a corkscrew to enjoy French wine.

My tent was compact but not water resistant.

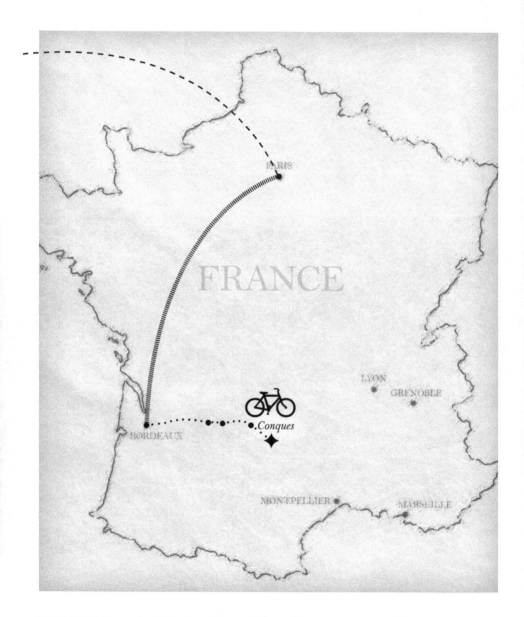

ROUTE NOTES: *Cycle from Saint-Céré to Conques, a major pilgrim center. Leave the valley of the Dordogne and travel along the River Célé and then the River Lot. Expect some steep hills to climb.*

DISTANCE: *52 miles or 84 kilometers*

Chapter 14

MYSTICAL CONQUES

y right knee aches, my legs are spent, and I'm saddle sore. Five days of riding have taken a toll. I'm not looking forward to a fifty-mile ride to Conques (pronounced "conk" with the *n* raised through the nose). While I have loved seeing France, the cycling has been more difficult than I imagined.

All the other cyclists have left, but I postpone my start as long as I can. I sit in the campground's computer center checking email, writing my blog, and downloading photos to my laptop. Wi-Fi, or "WEE-fee" as they call it in France, is cheap here, only one euro per half hour. I work until the support van is ready to set off.

Leaving the campground, I pedal slowly by myself uphill out of Saint-Céré. It's a long, gradual climb of about twelve miles. I ride easy, staying in my granny gear with high cadence. The "granny gear" is the smallest ring in a triple front chainring set. The moniker refers to the fact that it doesn't have many teeth.

It's another sweltering day, which compounds my fatigue. I try to keep moving but break in a dusty town along the way for water, peaches, and a Coca Light. The quiet rural roads pass through rolling green pastures with grazing cows. I stop my bike for a rest near the black-and-white bovines. They amble near me, eager for company.

Leaving the cows, I slowly ride the rolling hills for another forty-five minutes toward the River Lot. The final leg of the route provides a choice: a meandering ride along the banks of the Lot or a more difficult route that climbs above the Lot Valley into Conques. I opt for the easy route along the river bottom. Avoiding challenge is uncharacteristic of me, but my whole body aches.

I arrive in Conques hot and tired. I have afternoon tea, set up my tent, and watch a bit of the Tour de France. How strange to watch the Tour on television while I am in the very same country. I would love to see the riders pass by me live instead of listening to the rapid-fire French announcers. But I have my own tour to complete.

Following my television break, I primp for a stroll through the village and a group meal in town. This is a big deal because my hygiene during the bike tour has reduced itself to only the bare minimums: showering, shaving, and shampooing.

My hair is a mess. I lost my shampoo and conditioner three campgrounds ago. After that, I borrowed Nate's hair products once, but he stalked me until I gave them back. So I bought a substitute shampoo that sounded nice: *Orange et Miel pour Les Cheveux Normaux*, Orange and Honey for Normal Hair. Unfortunately, the shampoo smells like Mr. Clean and makes my hair look dry and straw-like. Besides, I didn't bring a hairdryer or straightener because of the different voltage in France. My hair looks frizzy after I wash it, and so I keep it pulled back in a ponytail at all times.

My civilian clothes typically look as unkempt as my hair. The cotton items that I dry in the sun become wrinkled beyond wear. Fortunately, I used a dryer and folded my cotton clothes carefully two nights before so I can look presentable.

I've decided to go all out tonight. I dress in my not-too-wrinkled khakis and pink t-shirt with a camisole underneath. I even dust on eye shadow, darken my lashes with mascara, and gloss my lips in a pretty pink shade. In a way, I feel foreign to myself. I've become so accustomed to biker wear and a face covered only in sunscreen.

I really like the self I'm becoming in France. I've morphed into a person *sans artifice*, or without pretense. All of the focus on appearances and meeting expectations can be exhausting. How refreshing to just *be*. In France I don't have the pressure to try to look beautiful. I knew no one when I arrived. No one cares about how I look, what I wear, or any other personal details. A smile, a warm conversation, and extending myself to another is all that matters here. And maybe that's all that matters anywhere. I've left behind my self-imposed critic and the expectations I perceive others have of me. The new me is content to ride a bike, explore the countryside, and meet new people along the way. No worries, except getting myself to the destination for the night and keeping my stomach filled.

After my complete grooming I walk toward Conques, passing by the Roman Bridge along the way. The stone bridge was constructed in the eighth century by the Romans, according to our tour notes. I'm set straight by Dominique, a good-natured, middle-aged man working in a garden by the bridge.

Dominique speaks some English, and he tells me that "Roman Bridge" is a misnomer. The bridge wasn't constructed by Romans, he explains, because the Romans weren't even in the country in the eighth century. He says the name was for Le Chemin de Saint-Jacques.

"That's the Path of Saint Jack in English," he says. "Jack was one of the disciples."

"Jack? A disciple named Jack? I don't think so."

"Yes," he insists. "There was a disciple named Saint Jack."

I'm not a religious scholar, but I do remember in Sunday school that I learned the twelve disciples of Jesus in alphabetic order: Andrew, Bartholomew, James, James, John, Judas, Matthew, Philip, Simon, Simon Peter, Thaddeus, and Thomas. No Jack. But I don't argue the point with Dominique.

Dominique explains that Conques is a stop along the Path of Saint Jacques, and that pilgrims can take one of many routes to Santiago de Compostela, Spain. This route starts in Rome, and that's why the bridge is called the Roman Bridge.

I leave Dominique and take a steep stairway into Conques. Sweat drips from my brow as I ascend the stone steps. I feel a stillness surround me as I climb beside medieval buildings, some of which have stood sentry for a millennium.

The village of Conques began near the end of the eighth century. A hermit called Dadon settled here, deciding it was a perfect meditation site. He later founded a community of Benedictine monks. Dadon named the village Conques, from the Latin word *concha* (shell), perhaps a name to fit the rocky terrain or the shell-shaped lay of the land.

At the same time that Conques was founded, the relics of Saint Jacques were uncovered in Compostela, Spain. Pilgrims soon began traveling to the shrine, and along the way, they would often visit smaller shrines. As legend has it, the monks at Conques wanted a way to attract some of these pilgrims—not to mention fame and riches. So they hatched a plan to pilfer some treasure and create their own village tourist trap. The monks knew that the relics of Sainte Foy, a virgin martyr, were stored at a monastery in Agen and so one of the Conques monks joined the frock in Agen. After ten years there, he stole the relics of Sainte Foy and brought them back to Conques.

Pilgrims 1,200 years ago flocked to see the relics of Sainte Foy. They still do today. More than 600,000 people visit Conques annually, most of them during the summer. They come to Conques to see the extraordinary architecture, religious relics, and spectacular natural surroundings. But there's so much more. While Conques is a treasured historical village, its magnificence is a palpable feeling of serenity. "Few places are known which speak more to the heart and spirit," the writer Henri Daniel-Rops said of Conques.

While tourists swarm during the day, at night the village is quiet. My first stop is the Abbey-church of Sainte Foy. It's a remarkable structure with meaning behind each intricate carving adorning the church's exterior.

Carved above the doors is a representation of "The Last Judgment." In the center of the scene is Christ, and angels and demons surround him, sorting through the souls of the dead. Roofed buildings with doors portray heaven and hell. In front of the Hand of God stands Sainte Foy, always ready to intervene on behalf of her people.

I stand back from the church to take a picture of the building. Before me I see what appears to be a family of five—a young couple and a young woman with grandpa and mom. Grandpa has his arm around the back of the female in the couple. The other young woman rests her elbows on the shoulders of grandpa and mom. Their heads tilt up, and they look up at the remarkable carving above the wooden doors to the church without saying a word. They seem in awe of the beauty. I stand about thirty feet behind them, and they don't notice me as I snap their photo. The exquisite carving is magnified by the family's reaction.

Inside, the church is cool compared to the steamy night air. I stroll through the aisle toward the front, looking at the Romanesque columns—212 in all. I sit in one of the pews, tilt my head back to look up, and stare at the expansive height of the ceiling. The abbey has a quiet resonance of tranquility.

By nature, I'm not a churchy-type person. I spent years as a new wife trying to establish myself as a churchgoer. My husband wasn't particularly religious either, but his parents were good Lutherans. I thought that if we could go to church together, we could form this happy family that I had always envisioned.

Though I enjoyed the people who attended church, I never found the deep connection to spirit I sought. Not so in the Abbey of Sainte Foy. I feel like the millions of prayers by the devoted have created a portal to the divine. This inspires me to give away my concerns, praying for the safe return of my cat, Oreo. (In her latest email, Alex told me that our cat has gone missing.)

After the serenity break at the church, I return to the cobblestone street to find the Visitor's Center in Conques to see when it opens. The Internet at the Conques campground is expensive, and I heard the Visitor's Center has reasonably-priced Wi-Fi access. I want to check my email to see if Alex had any word on the cat.

Near the Visitor's Center I meet a couple from Toulouse, a city famous for violets. They call themselves, in a very French accent, Row-BAIR and Ros-a-LEEN (Robert and Rosalyn). I jokingly pronounce their names in a heavy American accent: RAW-bert and RAW-za-lin. We all laugh. They don't speak English—but I manage to have an actual conversation in French about their vacation to Conques, a testament to my improving language skills.

I leave Robert and Rosalyn to meet the tour group for dinner. I can't wait to tell my tour group Dominique's story about the Roman Bridge. Drew, who has been to Conques many times before, tells me that he has never heard the story.

"Dominique also told me that the path is named after a disciple named Saint Jack."

"Jack? Do you mean Jacques?" asks Drew.

"Yes, he told me that Jacques is Jack in English."

Drew laughs. "No! Jacques is James in English. It's Saint James, not Saint Jack."

I'll never understand French.

Our dinner tonight is served on an outside patio. We feast on a five-course meal, including two dessert courses. Robert and Rosalyn walk by as we eat, and Robert cheerily says goodbye to me.

"Bonne nuit, Nancy."

"Bonne nuit, Row-BAIR et Ros-a-LEEN."

Several people at the table turn to watch the couple. They seem surprised that French strangers are wishing me good night. "Who are they?" David asks.

"Just some people I met," I say.

Robbie chuckles and shakes his head. "Found some more French people to adopt you, eh, Nance?"

The camaraderie, rich food, and warm summer night have left me contented. I smile as I imagine how tranquil I would feel staying here a while.

"I think I want to spend an extra day in Conques," I tell the group. "I'll just ride double the distance the next day."

"There's really not that much to see," says Ellie. "Maybe just spend the morning."

Ian has a different idea. "No, Nancy, you need more time than a morning. You should live here permanently. You can become a nun."

"A nun? What makes you think I want to be a nun?" I'm a bit insulted, but it is Ian saying this, and so I know that his intentions are probably good.

"It's the perfect solution for you. You could stay here and not worry about finding a man." He seems serious with this plan for me.

"I don't think things are *that* hopeless."

Or are they? Maybe that's what it has come to—living a celibate life in a nunnery. How depressing. But I'm not Catholic, I like having sex, and I prefer more fashionable clothing. True, I'm getting used to less primping, but I don't think I want to wear a scratchy black tunic every day and never have a manicure.

No, I think Ellie is right—a morning will do. I'll rise early to explore the village, starting with the golden statue and relics of the martyred girl saint.

An awe-inspired family views the Abbey-church of Sainte Foy.

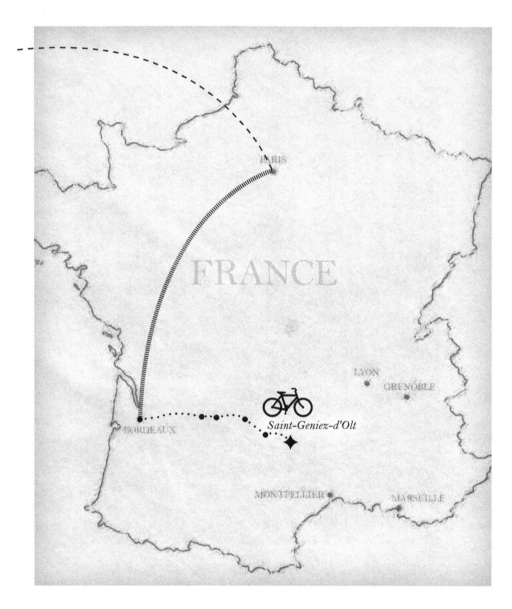

ROUTE NOTES: *Cycle from Conques to Saint-Geniez-d'Olt. Some climbing before a steep descent.*

DISTANCE: *55 miles or 89 kilometers*

Chapter 15

GOLDEN MOMENTS

W

ith more than fifty miles to ride today, I desperately need a way to ease my saddle-sore parts. Since I don't have butt butter, I use the only greasy substance I have: Vicks VapoRub. I rub it on in generous gobs. It feels better for a moment, until the menthol stimulation kicks in. Youch! The goop stings my delicate chafed skin like attacking hornets. What was I thinking? Has biking day after day caused temporary insanity?

After the Vick's sting has faded, I dress for the day and head for breakfast. I load a bowl with cereal, pile on freshly cut fruit and add milk. Then I grab a *pain au chocolat* and pour myself some coffee. Despite my gluttonous eating, my pants have started to sag.

I find a plastic chair under the canopy and sit next to Drew.

"Sleep well?" he asks.

"Not bad—I'm a little stiff," I say and roll my shoulders back to stretch them.

"It sounded like you slept well." He gives me his impish grin.

"What do you mean?"

Drew imitates a snore.

"Hey! That wasn't me."

He laughs.

In my tent, I finish packing my gear. And I can't believe it—my laptop is missing. Was it stolen? Or wait—I took it out at the campground in Saint Céré when I was checking email. I must have left it there. Damn. It's fifty miles away, in the other direction.

I can't call the campground. I don't remember the name and have no phone. Besides, would they even understand me? And then there's the issue of my two-wheeled transportation. It's a long way there and back. What am I going to do?

I'm embarrassed to tell anyone about my mistake, but I need help. I pull Drew aside.

"Something bad has happened."

"What is it?" he asks with concern in his voice.

"I think I left my computer at the last campground. Do you think you could call for me?"

Drew discreetly retrieves his phone and makes the call.

"You're in luck. It's there."

"Thank God. I'll ride back and pick it up."

"No, I'm driving the van today. I'll get it."

"That's too inconvenient for you."

"I'll put on some music, and it'll be a fun day of driving. Don't worry about it."

I'm feeling stupid for my mistake. This is such an imposition on poor Drew. His day will already be busy buying food for afternoon tea, hauling the luggage to our next campground, and setting up our canopy. Now he will also have to drive an extra two hours to our last campground because of my forgetfulness.

There's nothing I can do except get on with my day. I hop on my bike to ride a mile into the village. I had thought the steps into Conques were steep, but the road is even more of a challenge to ascend by bike. It must be a 10 percent grade. My legs are still heavy with fatigue, and I have a long ride ahead. I won't think about the rest of the ride until later.

For someone who likes to dwell on her thoughts, my new approach is a shift. I don't have the luxury of worrying—whether it's about a forgotten laptop, a challenging ride ahead, or my tumultuous dating life. My days are simple: pack up camp, ride, set up camp, shower, wash clothes, and go to bed (with many food and wine breaks in between).

Zen Buddhism teaches that the past is an illusion and the future is but a dream. And it dawns on me that most of my suffering in my dating life can be traced to not staying grounded in the present moment.

Jeff and I had dated for a month when I started imagining the details of our life together. Would we live in my house? His was too small and not in a great neighborhood. Maybe we could buy a new house together. How would he live with my dogs in the house? He hated that I let them stay inside.

I'm always making up endings to the romance novel, and when the story takes an unexpected twist, I'm devastated. Maybe all of these men have done nothing *to* me; I've done it to *myself.*

Arriving in Conques, my first stop is the Museum of Sainte Foy. The woman at the registration desk asks me something about Le Chemin de Saint-Jacques. Thanks to Dominique, I know what she's saying.

"*Oui,*" I proudly answer. "*Le Chemin de Saint-Jacques.*"

My smugness is short-lived as I realize I didn't understand the full message. She must have asked me if I was a pilgrim on the path. When I answered yes, she gave me a discount on the price of admission—four euros. I don't know how to correct the mistake, so I sheepishly take the discount and enter the museum.

The first part of the display includes old stone fragments and tapestries. I soon lose interest and make my way to the golden statue of Sainte Foy.

Sainte Foy, Saint Faith in English, was a young girl who was a devout follower of Jesus and lived in the third century AD. She wanted to help people in her village of Agen, and she would take food from her home to give to the poor. Her father didn't appreciate her altruistic nature, and one day, he demanded to see the food she had taken. Foy pleaded her innocence, and when she revealed what was hidden in her dress, the food had turned into flowers, just one of the many miracles chronicled about the girl. These frequent incidents became known as Foy's *joca*, Latin for "little jokes."

At the time, Romans ruled the land and practicing Christianity was against the law. No one knows why, but Foy's father turned her in to the Romans. He may have wanted to gain favor with the authorities or to scare Foy so much that she'd renounce her faith. The Romans were in a bind. They didn't want to kill a thirteen-year-old, but laws were laws. They told Foy that they would release her if she would just give up her religion and worship the pagan goddess Diana. Foy refused and defiantly told them that they could torture or even kill her, but she would never deny her beliefs. Her sister and other young Christians also turned themselves over, willingly sacrificing their lives for their forbidden faith. Eventually, the Romans beheaded the thirteen-year-old Foy, her sister, and all the young Christians.

The relics of Sainte Foy are called one of the five greatest medieval gold-plated treasures in Europe, according to a museum pamphlet I read. It also says that there is a piece of Sainte Foy's skull encased within the golden statue's head. I don't believe it; I must have misunderstood the French.

"C'est vrai? La tête de Sainte Foy est dans le statue?" I ask one of the museum staff if the head of Sainte Foy is in the statue—I don't know how to say "skull" in French.

"Oui. C'est vrai," she confirms.

As I walk into the darkened room, I see the golden statue which reminds me of a Hindu goddess rather than a Christian saint. The figure is about three feet tall and depicts Sainte Foy sitting in a chair. The band on her head and her dress are studded in precious gems. Her mouth turns down, giving her a solemn expression. Her dark-blue enamel eyes stare at me and seem to penetrate my soul.

She's stunning, and I'm in awe. Other people in the room seem equally enchanted. They speak in hushed voices, even though there's no reason to do so. I stand near the statue for a while and contemplate the greatness of a young girl who risked everything to stand by her beliefs.

Leaving the museum, I walk outside to relax and reflect in an open-air space with a large cross. I send out another prayer for my missing cat. Stories claim that Sainte Foy brought dead animals back to life. Maybe she can help with my kitty, Oreo.

We affectionately call Oreo the "man of the house." I'm not a cat person, and I resisted owning a cat even though Alex pleaded. Finally, right before her ninth birthday, Alex and I picked out Oreo, a one-year-old black-and-white tabby, from the animal shelter. Shortly after, my husband and I split, and Oreo became our "man."

Oreo was a restless feline. I tried to keep him indoors, but he would pace before open windows, begging me to take off the screen so he could taste freedom. He was miserable being inside. Despite my misgivings, I let him have his way. I discovered he was a hunter, climber, and acrobat. He'd often leave decapitated moles or dead birds just outside my bedroom. Occasionally, he'd even bring in a live bird, climbing up a tree to the second-story window of my room with a sparrow in his mouth. He'd let it go, and the scared bird would take flight in the house. I swear Oreo did this just to watch me frantically try to catch the flapping bird.

I grew to love the cat that I never wanted. He would jump on my bed at night and lay on my chest, purring with affection. He'd make me so hot that I'd eventually shove him off. Undeterred, he'd leap back on top of me. It was annoying—and endearing.

Before leaving town I ride to the visitor's center to check my email for news on Oreo, but there's no word from Alex. I stop for a *café au lait*. How wonderful the coffee tastes in French cafés, especially compared to the ground-infested coffee press variety I drink each morning at camp. By noon I'm leaving Conques and on the road.

I ride at a leisurely pace to Saint-Geniez and arrive by mid-afternoon. I'm hungry since I didn't eat lunch, so I ride through town in search of food. Along the way I see a group of gray-haired men playing a game on a dusty town square. Each man takes a turn rolling a metal ball toward a wooden ball about three feet away.

Curious, I park and lock my bike and walk toward the men. I find a bench directly behind them, and I sit. A man in a plaid shirt turns his head to look at me. I smile, and he turns back around. I imagine not many women in spandex watch the game.

I want to know what they are doing, and so I gather my courage and walk toward the men. Now several of them eye me suspiciously.

"Excusez-moi. Qu'est-ce que c'est?" I ask the man in the plaid shirt, pointing at the ball. The phrase "what is it" comes in handy during times like this.

He answers rapidly, and I tell him I don't understand. Other men are interested in what I want. They gather closer. The man in the plaid shirt repeats himself. I'm still not sure what he said.

"*Écrivez pour moi, s'il vous plaît.*"

The man pulls out a pen and writes the word down on a paper receipt that I pulled out of my back pocket.

PÉTANQUE

Another man says something to me in French. I tell him I don't understand. I'm American and only speak a little French. They smile, nod, and seem to like that I'm American. The plaid-shirt man calls over the only man in the group who speaks some English.

This guy is tall, which is not common with the Frenchmen I've seen. He looks to be in his seventies. He tells me he learned English fifty years before when he lived in India. He never practiced after he returned to France since no one he knew in Saint-Geniez spoke English—not until a strange American woman appeared at the village *pétanque* game.

He briefly explains the fundamentals of the game. The goal is to get the metal ball (called the *boule*) as close as possible to the small wooden ball called a jack (*cochonnet* in French, which means piglet). If one team lands close to the jack, other teams also have the option of using their turn to knock an opponent's ball out of play.

"Can I take photos?" I ask.

"Yes, of course."

The once wary men now frolic and laugh while they pose for the camera. My favorite subject is a rotund man with a blue-and-green-striped shirt and a beret. Another man rushes up to the big man and they dance in the dusty square. The others describe the big man as *gros ventre*, which they tell me means big belly.

Leaving the men, I ride my bike away from the town center. I find a *boulangerie* (bakery) and buy *pain avec jambon et fromage* (bread with ham and cheese) and a cookie. Next door is a bar, and I walk inside and sit on a stool. I order a glass of red wine and enjoy my meal while watching the Tour de France.

At about five in the afternoon, or *dix-sept heures* (seventeen hours) as they call it in France, I leave for the campground called Marmotel. It seems odd to me that a camp would be named after a marmot. Before I leave the next day, I must discover the origin of the name.

$\mathscr{B}$ICYCLE TOURING: MUST HAVES

- **Bicycle packed in bike case or box** – Frequent travelers may want to invest in a hard-shell case with wheels. For the more frugal traveler, visit your local bike shop and ask them to save one of the shipping boxes for new bicycles.
- **Bike supplies and tools** – Bring two spare inner tubes, one tire, patch kit, frame pump, floor pump, multi-tool, and tire irons.
- **Bike bag** – At a minimum, you'll want a bike bag for behind the saddle to store tubes, a patch kit, and tools. Other bags are available to stash a camera, sunscreen, and other personal items, or you can just stick these in your jersey back pocket.
- **Outer gear** – Bring a helmet and sweat band, sunglasses, rain jacket, gloves, and cycling shoes.
- **Clothes** – Bring a minimum of two jerseys, two pairs of cycling shorts and socks, plus arm and leg warmers.
- **Refueling products** – Include water bottles, sports drink powder, sports gel (my favorites are from Hammer Nutrition), energy bars, and electrolyte tablets.

- **For your comfort and convenience** – Spray-on sports sunscreen, SPF 30 or greater, works best. Also bring lip balm with sunscreen. A bike lock is essential. Find a small one that will fit in a back jersey pocket.
- **Butt butter** – It's also known as chamois cream. Don't forget this essential product!

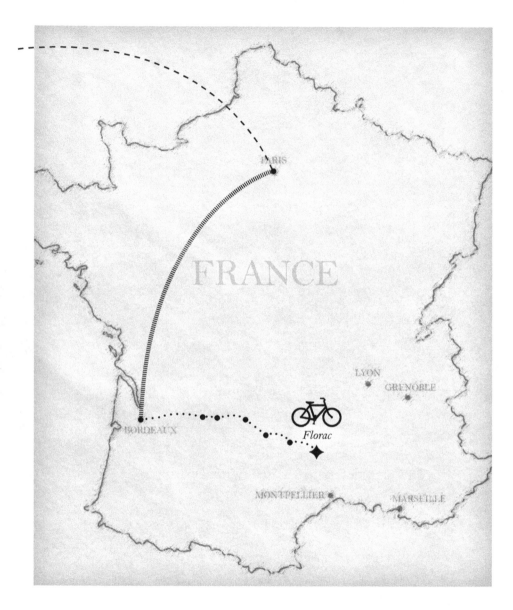

ROUTE NOTES: *Cycle from Saint-Geniez to Florac. Some climbing as we ascend the Col de Lagarde. Travel through the Gorges du Tarn with spectacular views.*

DISTANCE: *62 miles or 100 kilometers*

Chapter 16

INTO EACH LIFE
SOME RAIN MUST FALL

Snails are everywhere after last night's torrential downpour. Who knew snails could be two inches in diameter? I have only seen them tiny. Ian seems equally amazed; he puts his finger beside one to show that it's as long as the snail while I take a photo.

No wonder the French love to roast them and serve them with garlic and butter as escargot. Roasted snails have been eaten since prehistoric times throughout the Mediterranean. I could imagine some caveman, maybe Humphrey from the cave in Montignac, seeing a huge snail and thinking, *Hmmm...maybe it will taste good if I cook it over the fire.*

The French are the largest consumers of the gourmet appetizer, eating up to 40,000 tons each year. Much of this is imported, as the French are currently unable to produce enough snails to meet the demand.

Why not look for snails at campgrounds after a rainstorm? Snails from the wild can be collected and eaten, as long as you know which ones are edible. Some have an unpleasant taste. Others are poisonous.

The rain not only brought out the snails, it soaked my belongings. My Walmart tent is cheap and compact, but it's not water-resistant, as evidenced by my wet sleeping bag and pillow. The clothes I hung outside to dry are drenched. There's no time to deal with the mess. I'll have to dry everything tonight at the next campground.

Despite my wet beginning, my mood is upbeat. The sun is beginning to burn through the clouds, and I'm sure the weather report calling for rain is wrong. I'm optimistic that sun will prevail. I'm not the only one in good spirits. The birds are happy, chirping loudly in anticipation of their juicy worm breakfast.

More exciting than snails and birds is *free* Wi-Fi. Thanks to Drew, who brought back my computer yesterday, I can check my email in the reception area. Alex still has sent no word on the cat. I feel frustrated that I can't do anything so far away from home.

While I work on my computer, I notice one of the staff wearing a logo shirt for the Marmotel campground. Why would a campground be named after marmots? The women in the reception area don't speak English, so I converse in French using simple phrases.

"The people of Saint-Geniez are called marmots," says one of the women in French, whom I guess to be the manager.

"You mean like at a school—like a mascot?"

"No, all of the citizens of the village are called marmots."

I ask her why, and she gives me a brochure on Saint-Geniez-d'Olt that tells a legend from the end of the fifteenth century.

The brochure tells the story of two boys, sons of a Saint-Geniez fisherman, who kept a marmot at home as a pet. One afternoon a downpour began. The marmot ran away, and the boys chased after it. The storm became so severe that the river swelled and several houses, including theirs, were washed away. Their father and many others perished, but the boys survived thanks to the marmot. Thereafter, they were nicknamed "The Marmots" and now the name is applied to all the villagers.

Pétanque, snails, and marmots—I will never forget Saint-Geniez.

Our bike route today travels through Sévérac-le-Château—another medieval city with yet another castle. By the time I pedal there, Kate has already arrived in the van with Ellie. She seems eager to talk to me.

"Aren't you riding today?" I ask.

"It was too steep of a climb. I only like to ride when it's flat as a pancake."

I don't know how to respond. I want to roll my eyes, but I don't.

"I wanted to tell you about this American man who runs the shop down the street," she says. "He knows all about the history of this village. I thought you might be interested in meeting him."

"An American…here?"

"He's very fascinating. He has many old photographs and knows a lot of facts. I know how you like to find out about places, and I thought you might fancy meeting him." Despite her lack of cycling ambition, I do like Kate. It's thoughtful of her to think of me.I thank her and ride my bike to the shop. The first thing I notice is a sign: "English spoken here." This must be the place. The man standing behind the counter definitely doesn't look French with his dark blond hair and chubby cheeks. We introduce ourselves, and then I ask him about the history of Sévérac.

Todd tells me that people have lived continuously in Sévérac for more than 20,000 years attracted by the natural spring in the area. More than 1,000 years ago, the village started with the castle, Château de Sévérac. The remnants of the castle sit high above the village on a steep hill. Because the castle hadn't been kept in repair, it had crumbled through the centuries. Seeing opportunity in ruin, one previous owner had sold the rocks of the castle to townspeople to construct their houses.

"The street in front of the shop used to be a moat around the castle," Todd explains. "The buildings have only been here for the past hundred years or so."

He shows me an aerial view of the village, and from that vantage point, I can imagine where the moat had once been.

"My friend said you were American, but you sound Canadian."

"That's right! I'm originally from Thunder Bay, Ontario." I guess to the Brits, we North Americans all sound alike.

Random life decisions led Todd here. Canadians are known to speak French, but not in Todd's hometown of Thunder Bay. As an adult, he longed to speak the language and decided to attend an immersion school in France. While there, he met a French woman, and the couple continued a long-distance relationship when Todd returned to Canada. Eventually they married, and she agreed to move with him to Canada. Her paperwork was taking so long that Todd decided to try his luck at immigrating to France. In no time he had cleared the hurdles and moved with his wife to Sévérac where he started his shop.

I tried a long-distance relationship once. It didn't work out as smoothly as Todd's. Jim only lived across the state from me, not across the ocean, but we still needed a strong effort to make the relationship work. We met six years ago when he was in town for a softball tournament. The two of us had a combustible attraction for each other, which was a problem since he was still married at the time. I'm not proud to admit I fell for a married man. Soon after we met, he left his wife, and we started dating. Every two weeks we'd take turns driving five hours to see one another. In between visits we'd talk, and he'd send me cards. I still have the more than thirty cards and letters he sent to me. "My love for you grows each and every day," he wrote in one message. "I'm so glad you are in my life—you complete me," he wrote in another. Mostly, he'd tell me I was the love of his life.

If you met Jim, you'd wonder why I was so gaga over him. He wasn't especially handsome, he drank too much, and he needed constant reassurance. But I loved him dearly, and in hindsight, I can say it's because he loved me so much in return. I had never felt so adored in my life. We had talked about plans for our future. I tried to convince my daughter to move, but she was a freshman in high school and no way was she going for that. So the long-distance romance with Jim lingered. Over New Year's, a year and a half after we met, he surprised me with the news: he'd been seeing someone else.

It may sound pathetic that I took him back a few months later. I've heard many women say: "If he cheats on me, that's it. We're through." I used to say that myself. How could I become the stand-by-your-man kind of woman? My excuse is a hopeful heart.

I'm not saying this is a good thing. Most people who cheat will do it again. And true to form, Jim continued on with his philandering ways. My brain knew these things, but my hopeful heart had a mind of its own. It begged me not to let go of the love that made it feel alive. And with Jim, I let my heart talk me into giving him another chance. Then we broke up again. I didn't talk to him for a while, and he tried to win me back, even though he was engaged to another woman. He sent one last letter, sixteen pages declaring his eternal devotion. "I have never loved anybody as much as I love you, Nancy." Funny, he didn't think about that before he screwed around. This time I listened to my head, and I told him to get lost.

Still, if I had to do the relationship over, I'd do the same thing again. Despite being burned by Jim, I know that I at least took a chance on love. I never have to wonder what could have been.

After leaving Todd's shop, I decide to ride the steep path to the castle. Halfway up, I stop to see the natural spring fountain that's been providing fresh water to the area for 50,000 years. A sign says, "Place de la fountain," but all I see is a brick structure with a barred and locked gate. I dismount my bike, walk toward the gate, and peer into the darkness. I still don't see a fountain, but I do feel rain. A downpour begins. I squat in the doorway, watching the rain splatter down in big, noisy drops.

This weather is distressing. I really don't like riding in the rain. It wouldn't be so bad if I were inside listening to the drops pitter-patter on a roof. I might even find the rain relaxing, unless I was in a tin-roofed building.

That happened to me once. Alex and I were inside an old building in the ghost town of Virginia City, Montana (famous for the Vigilantes who took the law into their own hands). We were watching the Virginia City Players perform their variety act on stage when the rain and hail began. With the loud pops that sounded like gunfire, I thought the vigilantes had returned. It definitely was not a relaxing experience.

It's also not relaxing to be stuck in the middle of a rainstorm when you have to bike fifty miles. The poet Henry Wadsworth Longfellow wrote, "Into each life some rain must fall." I've had enough rain to last for a while.

After five minutes of waiting, I decide to skip the castle and seek cover at the village bar. Many other people had the same idea: the place is packed. I find a table and order a sandwich—a *croque-monsieur*, just like I had on the train to Bordeaux.

I wait for my lunch and watch people come into the bar. A biker seeking shelter walks in. He's a small, gray-haired man with a bright yellow rain jacket. He finds a seat in the back near me. Then some young men in their early twenties arrive. They stand by the bar and joke around with each other. More of their friends join them, and the men kiss each other on the cheek as a greeting. Their affection seems so natural here. It makes me think about how different things are in Montana. Don't get me wrong, people are friendly in the Wild West, but it's a place with more land than people. People have space to be left alone, and for the most part, they prefer it that way. It's not a place of public hand holding or hugging, and certainly not cheek kissing between men.

After I finish my lunch, the storm has lessened, but still it rains. The bartender speaks some English, and I ask him the French word for rain.

"La pluie," he says. *Pluie* sounds like "phooey," which is how the day is turning out.

The gray-haired cyclist leaves the bar. I should go myself. This is likely as good as it will get, and I have a long ride ahead. Before I leave, I take out two plastic grocery bags I had stashed in my jersey pocket. Removing my shoes, I slip the plastic bags as a barrier between my socks and shoes. At least my feet should stay warm this time.

Out in the rain, I hop on my bike and pedal rapidly. My legs are really feeling better today. I gradually climb out of town, and I see the bright yellow jacket of the cyclist from the bar. He becomes a target for me. He pedals a little harder as I near him. Maybe he doesn't want to be passed, but I do so anyway, and it feels good. Welcome back, ego.

The man won't be dropped. As I ride on, I turn my head from time to time and notice that he keeps nearby. The ride leads through the Gorges du Tarn, and when I stop to take a picture, the man closes the gap. He slows down to check if I need help, and when he sees my camera out he waves as he rides past. I think he's happy that a woman didn't outride him. I wonder where he's from and where he's going, but I'll never know. That's how it can be on life's journey. Some people share your path for a moment, leaving before you've had a chance to even become acquainted.

Our tour notes say that the views are spectacular on this day of riding. Still, I'm unprepared for the dramatic beauty of the Gorges du Tarn. From my vantage point, the River Tarn seems far below. The gorge took millions of years to create, caused by water eroding the limestone cliffs. These dramatic gashes are the deepest gorges in Europe and in some places, plunge 500 meters deep, the equivalent of five-and-a-half American football fields. The area also provides sanctuary for native plants, wildflowers, and vultures. I don't have the patience to stand here any longer admiring this natural wonder in the pouring rain, so I get back on my bike and pedal strongly toward camp.

Today, I'm not as cold as last time I rode in the rain. I'm wearing my waterproof jacket and knee warmers, and plastic bags have kept my feet dry. Still, there's something demoralizing about riding in a downpour. I'm feeling cranky about the weather by the time I near the campground in Florac. Just as I think how much I hate the rain, I see the welcoming sign of a hotel. My imagination runs wild. I could sleep in a bed, have a shower to myself, and maybe even watch some TV that I don't understand. I'm sick of roughing it. This is supposed to be *my* vacation, and I don't want another night sleeping in a wet tent. What was I thinking when I signed up for two weeks of camping?

Before I can go to the hotel, I'll have to wash and dry my wet sleeping bag, pillow, and clothes. Everyone else has the same idea, and I wait my turn to use the washer and dryer. A French woman is first in line, then David, and finally me. David agrees to put my wash in after he's done with his. That cheers up my mood, but only for a moment.

I'm irritated that there's no indoor restaurant at the campground, only an outside café with a tin roof. It's just drizzling now, so I won't have to listen to pounding rain. But now that I've stopped, I feel cold. I can't change because all my clothes are wet, waiting to be washed and dried.

I might as well eat. I'm tired of ham, so I order a *saucisson* (sausage) sandwich and *frites,* or French fries. (It's an ironic name since the potato originated in South

America. No one knows for sure who first deep fried the spud. Both the French and Belgians claim that one of their own first created fries.) I sit at a table by myself near some French people. A little white terrier dog comes near me. It's been a while since I've seen a dog. I wonder how Lucky and Zimmer are doing. Alex hasn't reported any escapes lately.

"Sit." I say. The little dog doesn't respond.

"How do you say 'sit' in French?" I ask one of the nearby patrons whom I heard speaking some English. He tells me the word.

"Asseyez!" (pronounced "ah-say-YAY") I command the dog. The terrier sits. I give him a fry.

I ask the man how to say "lie down," and he tells me.

"Couchez!" ("coo-SHAY") I order. The dog lies down. He's rewarded with another fry. I laugh and clap. At least the *dog* understands my French.

The dog cheers me up, and so does David. He not only washed my clothes, he threw my loads into the dryer and folded everything. It's nine and my wash is complete. Drew also helps my disposition by suggesting I set my tent up under the canopy to keep out of the rain. That sounds easier than riding my bike back with a backpack down the road to the hotel. As I snuggle in my freshly washed sleeping bag, I realize that despite the challenges, I feel content to be experiencing my dream of riding my bike in France.

I've always longed to share my life journey with someone. Now I realize that I'm satisfied living this adventure on my own. It rains all night in Florac, but I stay dry under the canopy. With the help of my friends, I found a way out of the storm.

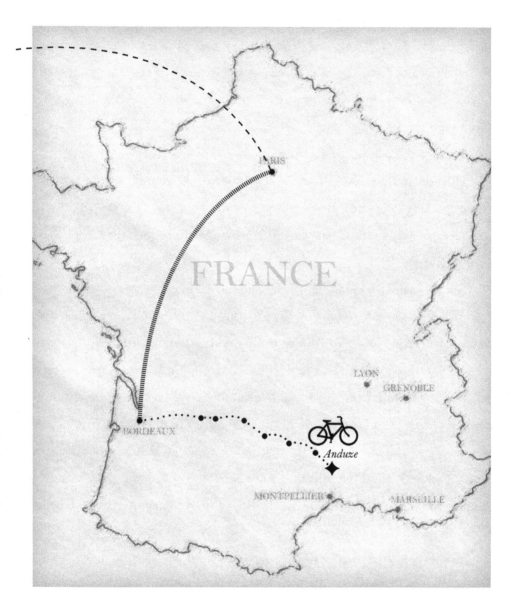

ROUTE NOTES: *Cycling from Florac to Anduze. It will be a short day of riding with views in the Cévennes mountains. Wine suggestions: the powerful reds of Côtes du Rhône and the crisp rosés of Provence.*

DISTANCE: *44 miles or 71 kilometers*

Chapter 17

THE OLD LADY IN
LE POMPIDOU

As I start on the road from Florac to Anduze, I have one goal in mind: to get through the ride. While the weather has improved, my knee is bothering me again. Maybe it's my lackluster attitude, but I find the ride tedious and have no interest in stopping. My mindset changes when I see an old lady walking out of her house toward the street in the small village of Le Pompidou. The woman moves slowly using a cane. Other people wait for her by a car. Maybe it's her family taking her to church on this Sunday morning.

I spot her from a block away, and I slow my bike as I near her. She looks to be in her mid-eighties with her creased face and thick crown of white, wavy hair. A robin's egg blue dress drapes over her ample figure. A gray vest covers the dress, providing some protection from the chilly morning air. She wears thick stockings and heavy black shoes. I bring my bike to a standstill across the street from the old lady in Le Pompidou.

"*Pardonnez-moi. Je voudrais une photo de vous, s'il vous plaît,*" I say.

She stops in her tracks and nods at my request for her photo. I snap her picture as she ponders the stranger clad in a bright yellow jacket. Her younger companions wait for her by the car. She resumes walking, passes them, and stops five feet away from me, standing in the street. She talks in French at a measured pace, and I understand.

"*Pourquoi voulez-vous ma photo?*"

How can I explain? I know how to say I'm American and want photos. But it's more than that. I want to capture the world of France I'm discovering. I'm just not sure how to put it all together.

"*Je suis américaine. Je voudrais les photos de tout le monde en France où je visite. Comprenez-vous?*"

The woman considers my awkward sentence and pauses for a moment before responding.

"*Oui, je comprends,*" she finally says. She understands.

She gives me just a hint of a smile. Assisted by her cane, she ambles back to the car where her family waits. I mount my bike and pedal out of the village of Le Pompidou. I wave to her as I ride away.

Everyday events like an old woman walking in a French village become refreshing slices of life through my tourist eyes. I loved meeting that old lady in the blue dress, and now I can see her again and again.

My only regrets with photos are the ones I didn't take. I missed a photograph of people young and old splashing in the water at Miroir d'Eau in Bordeaux. I didn't take one of the young woman who rode a bike with a basket filled with baguettes. I passed right by two elderly ladies who sat on a bench in the French countryside enjoying a gentle breeze on a hot summer evening. These memories are fragments now, not vivid mind pictures like the images I have captured with my compact camera.

Regrets are of no use without growing into new patterns. I'm learning to stop and observe, immerse myself in the people and places before me, and enjoy the beauty in every moment. I'm capturing the essence of my experience by taking photos, writing down my experiences, and sharing my discoveries with my tour companions every night. This way, my French journey will live long after my travels end.

The ride on this day travels through the cols, or mountain passes, from Florac to Anduze. I travel by myself through the sparsely populated villages and back roads. Slowly, I climb up the cols, taking it easy for the challenge ahead. In two days we will ride up one of the steepest climbs in the world, Mont Ventoux.

Our campground for the evening is located in Anduze, which our tour notes say is the official beginning of Provence. I watch the Tour de France on the campground television with some of my cycling companions. Australian rider Cadel Evans takes over the yellow jersey and is now the overall leader of the Tour de France. Some of my Aussie friends are so jubilant, they break out in cheer.

"Aussie, Aussie, Aussie! Oi, Oi, Oi!"

"Aussie, Aussie, Aussie! Oi, Oi, Oi!"

Over and over they cheer with national pride. I'm surprised and amused by their chant. It's like Americans shouting, "U.S.A! U.S.A!" Still, I wonder, what would the old lady from Le Pompidou think? Or what about the other French people I had met along the way?

The French culture is so dissimilar from what I know back home, and obviously unlike the Australian culture as well. Maybe the language makes a difference.

When I had my French lessons with Patrick, the bartender in Bordeaux, he told me that French was a romantic language. Now the formal definition of a romance language is that it derived from Latin. Patrick said there was more to it than that. If I wanted to speak French, I needed to understand that the present tense of French can represent more than something going on at the time of speaking. "When you say 'I love you' in French, you say 'I love you in the past. I love you now. I love you forever.'"

He was trying to explain that literal translations won't work. If I wanted to expand my language repertoire, I needed to start thinking like a French person. It makes me wonder, how does a language affect a culture? Could I really only understand a culture by mastering the language? Or maybe it's the other way around. I'll never understand the language unless I immerse myself in the culture.

With only a week and a half left in France, I doubt that I will suddenly become fluent in the language. But maybe I can work on appreciating French culture through my experiences. Tomorrow will provide the perfect opportunity as July 14 marks Bastille Day, the celebration of the country's independence.

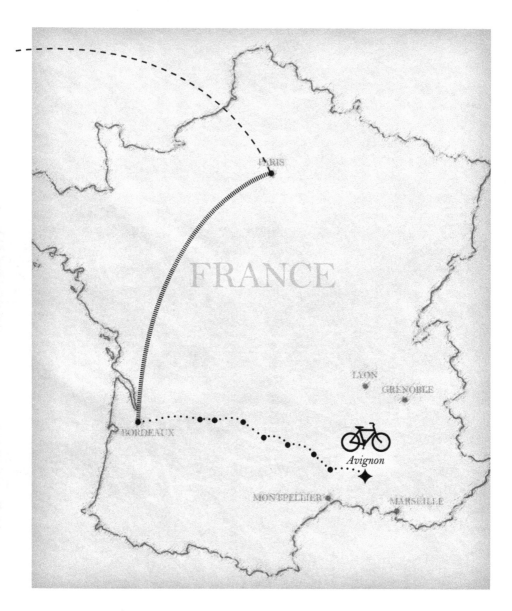

ROUTE NOTES: *We're officially in Provence. Cycle from Anduze to Avignon. Travel through Uzès and Pont du Gard, the ancient Roman aqueduct.*

DISTANCE: *66 miles or 106 kilometers*

Chapter 18

KISSES
ON BASTILLE DAY

R iding through the village of Anduze, I see a crowd gathered. Children, teenagers, and adults of all ages form a semicircle facing a platform in front of a building. Policemen stand near the crowd. They wear friendly expressions and are dressed formally in blue slacks, white short-sleeve shirts with insignias, and round hats with flat tops called *képis*.

From the balcony of the building, three blue, white, and red national flags of France flap in the wind. (Never say "red, white and blue" to describe the French colors.) The tricolors represent the ideals of the French Revolution: freedom, equality, and fraternity. Just in case someone missed the subtle message from the flags, the words *"Liberté, Égalité, Fraternité"* are inscribed in large black letters on the building.

The townspeople listen to an official-looking young woman who stands on the platform and speaks into a microphone. She wears a pantsuit with a blue, white, and red sash draped around her, like a Miss America contestant without the state's name emblazoned on the satin. Next to speak is a man in a gray pin-striped suit and the same Miss America sash. They talk too rapidly for me to comprehend. I ask a man near me if he speaks English. Benoit (pronounced "ben-WAH") explains the scene. Students from the local school are being honored for their academic achievements, and the leaders of the town's library are conducting the ceremony. This must be a Bastille Day tradition.

Following the speeches, Benoit invites me for a drink. The library is serving *apéritifs*. Drinking at the library? We never did that back home. "No thanks," I say, even though it's Bastille Day. The day is still early, and I have a long ride ahead. I wish Benoit *au revoir*. He surprises me with a kiss.

Benoit is thin, gray-haired, and bespeckled. Not the dream man I envisioned for my first French kiss. He kisses me twice—on each cheek. *Deux fois pour les bons amis.* Two times for good friends. What other surprises await me on Bastille Day?

Much like Americans celebrate their independence on the Fourth of July, the French celebrate their independence every July 14 with a national holiday complete with parades, picnics, and fireworks. It's called *Fête Nationale* (National Celebration) in French, but English speakers call it Bastille Day. On July 14, 1789, the French people stormed the Bastille, a prison that represented the oppression of the French monarchy. Considering it's a national celebration, it's ironic that only seven prisoners were jailed in the Bastille at the time. But the event meant more than the prisoner's release: storming the Bastille symbolized liberty and the fight against oppression for all French citizens, marking the start of the French Revolution. Think of it as the Boston Tea Party, but more violent.

By the time I leave the celebration and Benoit in Anduze it's lunchtime. I don't want to eat lunch before my ride begins, but a snack will be OK. I see a fruit stand on the outskirts of Anduze and buy three peaches. I eat two at the stand and put the other in my back pocket. Today I feel like I might have *la pêche.* I feel well rested and ready to roll.

Our riding notes claim we have entered Provence. As I ride out of Anduze, I don't see any difference from the countryside on rides from previous days. Then a few miles down the road, the magic of Provence blooms forth. Expansive fields of sunflowers reach toward the sun. I stop my bike and capture their amber heads with yellow fringe as they bob toward the light. Taking photos of sunflowers provides a needed diversion to take it easy, which is sometimes difficult when you have *la pêche.* My plan is to ride leisurely to save my legs for the big climb up Mont Ventoux tomorrow. A massive tailwind helps me sail down the road without much effort.

By mid-afternoon, I'm in Uzès and my stomach begs me to stop for lunch. I ride to the town center and stop at an outdoor café.

"Qu'est-ce que vous voulez?" The waiter asks what I want in a gruff voice.

"Je voudrais du pizza. Quelle sorte avez-vous?" He becomes even more annoyed. He opens my menu for me and points to the listings of pizzas. Then he huffs away.

"Don't worry about him. They are very busy here because it is Bastille Day," says a man sitting at the table next to me.

He speaks in perfect English with a French accent. He lights up a cigarette, and I notice that he's even older than Benoit. The man is with a woman, probably twenty years younger than him, who speaks English with an American accent. Her name is Jessica, and her husband is named Jean.

The waiter returns, and I order pizza and wine. I can always count on pizza here, which I've tried on several occasions. It's entirely different from the overstuffed monsters back home. The crusts are thin and chewy, spread with a brushing of marinara sauce or olive oil, and topped with tangy local cheeses. The topping choices include fresh tomatoes, onions, olives, mushrooms, and sausage. The twelve-inch pizzas are served whole and uncut. And since I'm in France, where eating with fingers seems uncouth, I always use a fork and knife to cut my pizza into bite-sized pieces.

As I eat my pizza, I talk to Jessica and Jean. I learn how they met, why they moved to the U.S., and why they are back in France. Jessica is an artist, capturing life in Provence. Some of her paintings are inside the restaurant, and she leads me inside to see them. I particularly admire one of an old building, which Jessica tells me was once a laundry house that's just down the road.

"Would you like to see it?" she asks.

Why not? I wish her husband *au revoir*—and he gives me French kiss number two.

"Trois fois pour les très bons amis," he says as he kisses my cheeks three times since I am now a very good friend. He then switches to English. "If you ever want to return, you can stay with us in Uzès."

Jessica and I walk to the old laundry house. The place is in disrepair and boarded up, but we peer through the slats. The village women had once used the building as their laundry house. Instead of washing machines, the women used a large tub that looks like a wading pool. Jessica thinks the building is owned by a duke who lives in Uzès.

"Didn't the royalty system die with the French revolution?"

"Yes, it did," Jessica says, "but some families were able to keep their property and still use the titles." The duke also owns the castle in town, which she points out to me.

We walk back to the restaurant, and Jessica and I say goodbye, exchanging cheek kisses. I hop on my bike and ride toward the Pont du Gard—the bridge of an ancient Roman aqueduct.

Considered France's best-preserved portion of the Roman aqueduct, the Pont du Gard was built to move water from a spring near Uzès to Nîmes. In 38 AD, construction on the aqueduct began and reached completion fourteen years later. The effort required the labors of a thousand men to assemble more than 50,000 tons of stone, with some stones weighing six tons each. The aqueduct is considered an astonishing engineering accomplishment, especially for the time, because each of the stones was precisely cut to fit together without mortar. Jessica told me that she had once taken a class on the Pont du Gard and learned that the aqueduct had not been successful in the long term because minerals in the water continually clogged it up. When the Romans left, no one else knew how to remove the residue. Eventually, it became unusable.

Today, the Pont du Gard is flooded with people enjoying a day of sightseeing on a national holiday. It's late, and I don't feel like getting off my bike to explore the aqueduct. I ride down the pathways instead, trying to avoid hitting tourists. After my quick tour, I start toward the campground.

It's an ugly ride from Pont du Gard to the campground outside of Avignon. I travel on a busy highway through an industrial area filled with traffic. A headwind and hills make the going slow. I arrive at camp by seven, just as some of the tour group is leaving in the van toward Avignon. Tonight we will celebrate Bastille Day near the palace of the second pope.

Second pope? It's true. While Rome has long been home to the Catholic pope, for a period lasting a bit more than a century the pope lived in Avignon. The year 1305 saw the beginning of the papacy of Clement V, a Frenchman. The Romans disliked him, however, and for four years he suffered their cold shoulder. By 1309, he had had enough and moved the papacy to Avignon. The popes who succeeded Clement V remained there for seventy years. Then, in 1377, Gregory XI decided to give Rome a try. Unfortunately, the Romans weren't much friendlier with him. He considered moving back to Avignon but died and never made it.

The cardinals in France were bothered by Gregory's return to Rome. They also despised his successor, Urban VI, whom they considered to be hostile to their interests. In response, thirteen of the French cardinals voted to elect another pope, and for the next four decades, the Romans and the French each had their own pontiff.

The Palais des Papes (the pope's palace) in Avignon is the largest Gothic palace in Europe, spanning more than two and a half acres. The building hosts a museum, an exhibition hall, and a collection of frescoes. Surrounding the palace is Place du Palais (palace square), a neighborhood that was originally established by Romans more than two thousand years ago and today is a public square.

Nate, Drew, and I are the last to depart the campground, and our mission is to find a place to eat. When we arrive, we walk through the narrow streets of Place du Palais lined with shops and restaurants. The area is jam-packed with people attending the Avignon Festival where visitors watch theater performances, listen to music, or see other live events.

All the restaurants are full with hour-long waits for a table, but we're in luck. We see Ellie and Jack at a Vietnamese restaurant, and the three of us join them.

Our dinner consists of little appetizers and wine, endless wine. After dinner, we switch to sake when the owner of the restaurant arrives outside with a bottle of the Japanese rice wine. We drink out of ceramic shot glasses that come with a surprise: when filled a nude image appears at the bottom. It's so novel that we all keep our glasses topped off.

I should have stopped drinking before the sake. I didn't. I definitely should stop drinking after we leave the restaurant. I still don't. I follow my friends to a bar and we order another round, a mojito for me. We drink, dance, laugh, and take photos of our Bastille Day celebration.

At midnight we leave the bar. Ellie is still perky and chirpy. She wants to shoe shop. I feel sick and dizzy. I want to puke.

"I need to go," I tell Drew.

Drew finds us a cab back to camp. When we arrive, I change into sweat pants and a t-shirt. I take out my contacts and leave my face dirty and my teeth unbrushed. I crawl into my sleeping bag and pass out. I'm too drunk to worry about tomorrow's torturous ride up Mont Ventoux.

Ahhhh....Provence!

$\mathcal{T}$OP TEN CLIMBING TIPS

by Andy Applegate, Pro Level Coach with
Carmichael Training Systems

1. **Train!** Yup, simple as that. Ride more and train with a plan and your climbing will improve. You can be as methodical with it as you want, but even a little bit of structure and forethought will go a long way.

2. **Lose weight if you have it to lose.** I know you hate to hear it, but most of us are carrying at least a little extra body weight that we have to lug up the hills. Climbing is all about power-to-weight ratio. To go faster you can get stronger, get lighter, or both. You do need to be careful here as you don't want to lose too much weight (in which case you will lose power as well) or do it too quickly. Most riders who embark on a serious training plan and pay attention to improving their nutrition will see a gradual decrease in body fat leading towards their optimal riding weight and body

composition. Even losing a couple of pounds can make a big difference in climbing speed.

3. **Stay seated most of the time while climbing.** Especially on long climbs, unless you are very small and light, most riders are more economical when they climb seated. You can waste somewhere between ten and fourteen watts of power by standing. This is not to say you shouldn't get out of the saddle from time to time to work the muscles a little differently, stretch out the legs, or accelerate, but work on climbing primarily seated.

4. **When you do stand on a climb, keep your weight back over the saddle rather than jumping forward over the front of the bike.** You should not have much weight on your hands, allowing you to put a large amount of your body weight into each pedal stroke.

5. **Relax your upper body.** Any unnecessary tension in muscles that are not helping propel the bike forward is wasted energy. Consciously try to relax your face, neck, shoulders, back, and arms. Let your muscles from the hips down do all the work.

6. **Love the challenge.** If you hate to climb, you will probably never be good at it. Mentally embrace the challenge of defeating gravity with every pedal stroke and know that at the top you will be greeted with a sense of accomplishment, and maybe even a great view and fun downhill ride on the other side.

7. **No hills where you live?** Use headwinds to simulate the resistance of climbing. If you train inside, raise your front wheel from time to time during workouts to simulate climbing.

8. **Ride a steady pace.** Many riders will go too hard at the bottom of a climb and "blow up" far before it is complete, causing them to suffer and slow down. Take it easier on the lower slopes and increase the effort as

you go, cresting strong. This will give you the fastest time up the climb and leave you feeling much better about it.

9. **Ride a comfortable cadence.** Use the cadence comfortable for you. Don't be afraid to shift those gears and use the easy ones to give you a cadence that will allow a balance between muscular and cardiovascular stress. Experiment while riding to see what gearing and cadences you are comfortable with on various grades. There is nothing wrong with mounting easy gears on the bike if you know you are going to be doing long or steep climbs. Triple chainring, compact cranks, and a variety of rear gearing choices are available.

10. **Have fun.** If you are having fun you will enjoy all your time on the bike whether the route is uphill, downhill or flat.

Contact Andy Applegate via email: aapplegate@trainright.com

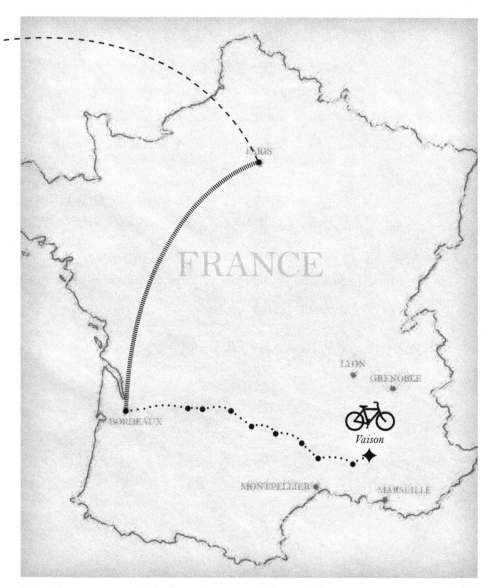

ROUTE NOTES: *Cycle from Avignon to Vaison. There are two routes available: one through the wine town of Châteauneuf-du-Pape and Orange; the other over Mont Ventoux. This legendary mountain is one of the hardest, hottest, and windiest mountains that you can climb by bicycle.*

DISTANCE: *68 miles or 109 kilometers*

Chapter 19

THE GIANT
OF PROVENCE

I should have been worried about riding up Mont Ventoux. It's one bitch of a climb: fourteen miles up a mountain with an average gradient of 7.5 percent. I wake up at six with my head throbbing and my stomach feeling quaky. I lie still, hoping that my queasiness will go away. Why did I drink so much last night?

Two hours later I still feel sick. How will I ever ride up a mountain? Maybe a cold splash of water on my face will help. I leave my tent and see Simon.

"Good morning," he says.

"Ehhh," I grunt.

He stops and stares. "What's wrong with you?"

I just keep walking to the bathroom. The splash doesn't help. I still feel sick. I return to the campsite and find a chair under the canopy. I look at the pile of

French pastries and the thought of eating makes me feel even more nauseous. I pour a cup of water and slowly drink. I set my left elbow on the chair's arm and rest my head on my hand.

"You look terrible," says Simon. I don't look up but I recognize his highbrow British accent.

"Thanks," I say, without making eye contact. Simon is right, I must look like hell.

"Did you take a nudging, Nance?" asks Robbie.

"A nudging?" I don't know what he means.

"Did you drink too much?"

"Yeah," I answer quietly. I look up and notice that everyone is staring at me now.

Nate chimes in: "You'd better eat something."

Mostly, I ignore Nate's advice. He has been nagging me for days to eat more. I think he eats like a buffalo, but I keep my opinion to myself. Today, though, he is right. I need something in my stomach to ease the gurgling acid inside. I pick up a dry baguette, tear off a small hunk, and chew slowly. I wash the bread down with water.

How can I ride at all—let alone up Mont Ventoux? I'm really worried. How stupid to drink so much before this ride. Why isn't everyone else sick too? Nate didn't drink much, but Drew, Ellie, and Jack consumed as much alcohol as me— maybe more. They seem fine, eating their cereal and pastries while I chew on this dry baguette.

I'd like to take Kate's usual place in the van. For once she's cycling, but she's not going up Ventoux. She and Simon are taking the easier route through Châteauneuf-du-Pape. But I can't just skip the ride. I've told all my cycling buddies back home, most of whom are men, about my epic climbs. How can I face them if I don't even try?

"Why don't you just start and see how you feel," suggests Drew. The ride to the base of the mountain is flat, he tells me.

With trepidation, I mount my bicycle and head toward the mountain. I'm surprised that as I pedal with the group out of Avignon, I start feeling a little better—not great, but at least not queasy. Then I notice Mont Ventoux looming in the distance, and my stomach feels uneasy again. The mountain is known by many names: Bald Mountain, Tour of the Moon, and Windy Mountain. I think the name Giant of Provence seems most fitting. Although the mountain is part of the French Alps, it is isolated by itself in Provence; its white head dominates the landscape.

After riding thirty miles, we arrive in Bédoin where we stop for lunch. I have a ham and cheese baguette, a Coke Light to help perk me up, and lots of water. While some of the others start on their ride, I shop for replacement cleats at the bike shop. Walking on cobblestone and bricks has taken a toll on my shoes, making clipping into my pedals difficult. This could pose a problem. If I have to stop while ascending Mont Ventoux, I might not be able to clip back in. If this happens, I won't be able to start pedaling. And then what? Would I fall over? Roll backwards? I don't want to find out.

I can't put it off any longer: it's time to take on the challenge. Gradually, I climb out of Bédoin toward the mountain. This isn't too bad. I don't know why I was so worried. I concentrate on Coach Jay's hill-climbing advice: "Keep a high cadence and ride easy. You'll wear your legs out if you grind a low gear."

After a few miles, the terrain becomes abruptly steep. I ride in my smallest granny gear, and I can barely peddle. I forget about Coach Jay and find something new to think about: Dante. I picture him writing the text message. He must have written me because deep down he really does care. But if he cared he wouldn't want to date other women, and certainly, he would have sent at least one email by now.

The thoughts of him aren't helping. I'm in a lot of pain. My shoulders and neck feel stiff, my quadriceps are killing me, and my bottom is chafed from riding day after day without chamois cream. I just bought some butt butter at the Bédoin cycling shop and spread the greasy lubricant on in the dressing room. It won't eradicate the rash already there.

After a mile and a half, I'm breathless and stop when the road's steepness subsides. I consider turning back. This is the easy part of the climb; at some points, the climb can reach a 9 or 10 percent gradient. That means nine miles of even harder climbing ahead. How can I make it to the top?

While I rest my throbbing head on my handle bars, Beth passes me. Then a lanky teenager leaves me behind. I hate being the weak sister.

I give myself a pep talk. You can do it, even if it means stopping every mile for a break. I get back on my bike, and thank God, I can clip in. I ride sideways on the road to gain momentum. This time I pedal two miles without stopping. I catch my breath again and resume the grind to the top. Strangely, the more I ride, the more my legs and mind become used to the rigors of riding up a mountain.

The bottom part of Mont Ventoux is a hot, humid forest. Its lushness is surprising considering that by the late 1700s the forest had been decimated after centuries of harvesting timber and overgrazing. To escape the oppressive heat I ride in the shade of trees whenever possible. I not only have to deal with the heat but relentless flies. Normally, flies are not an issue when riding, but I'm going so slowly that flies circle, land, and bite. Sometimes I try to blow on them or brush them off. They return to hassle me some more.

About two-thirds up the mountain, the forest disappears and all that remains is a bare, white, rocky mountaintop. I've heard this is the difficult part of the ride, but it seems easier to me. The air is cooler, the flies have disappeared, and the occasional switchbacks provide flat spots that allow my legs fifteen seconds of recovery time.

Beth is out of site, but the lanky teen sticks nearby. He rides stronger up the mountain, but he takes more frequent breaks than I do. Maybe I can pass him after all. Drew drives the support van for the day. He sees me as I ride up the moonscape terrain.

"You're spinning well," he says. "You're looking really good."

He takes a few photos, and I give him a thumbs-up. Maybe he's lying, but his animated voice makes me smile and renews my energy. Other riders also encourage me. As they descend, many give me a thumbs-up or say *"Allez!"* (Go!) as they pass. Words of support are also written on the road. *"Allez, Monique,"* someone has written for a rider. I pretend the words are meant for me, not Monique.

I'm ahead of the lanky cyclist now, and I keep pedaling. A professional photographer standing beside the road snaps some photos. This time I keep my focus fixed ahead. As I near the top, a car in front of me stalls. I'm on a 10 percent grade, and if I stop now, I know starting again will be a problem.

"Go!" I yell, forgetting that I'm in France. The car starts just as I reach the point of having to veer around it, sparing me from the risk of riding into oncoming traffic.

Near the top is a memorial littered with water bottles honoring Tom Simpson, an English Tour de France rider who died while riding up the mountain. Before ascending Mont Ventoux for the 1967 Tour de France, Simpson took amphetamines and drank half a bottle of cognac. I wouldn't advise this as a preparation for Ventoux. (You should also avoid drunken binges the night before.)

I see some cyclists who have stopped to pay tribute at Simpson's memorial. The lanky cyclist rides by me, saying *"Nous l'avons fait!"* Yes, we made it. I don't feel upset that he passes me. I'm grateful I'm almost done with the ride.

I take a wrong turn at the mountain crest. Beth comes down to tell me that I need to go up one more incline—about a hundred feet—to the end. She holds me steady as I clip back in my bike to tackle the last steep climb.

I make it to the top and see the friends who have arrived before me. They're clapping and cheering me on. I feel like one of the contestants finishing *The Amazing Race*. It's a magical moment. Mont Ventoux is the highest point for miles around, and the views are breathtaking. I feel like bursting out in tears; I'm so happy and relieved.

Twenty minutes later, our oldest rider, Ian, is nearing the top on a double crankset. This means he is riding a bike with a middle and high gear range, but no granny gear. Because of this, pedaling takes much more effort for Ian.

Less than a year ago, Ian was told he might die of a blood clot, and so he started taking blood thinners. Even with the treatment, doctors told him that recovery was not certain. He might never walk again, or worse, his leg might have to be amputated. Ian had other plans: he was convinced that if he could cycle again, his leg would improve. And a vision formed for him to return to France to cycle. Now here he is, nearing the summit of a massive mountain on his bicycle. He's the inspiration of the day for me and my fellow riders. We cheer him as he closes in on the final stretch: "Aussie, Aussie, Aussie! Oi, Oi, Oi!"

We all made it up that wicked mountain. Drew takes a photo of us on top of Mont Ventoux. Our smiles show the radiance in our spirits at having conquered this mountain. For most of us, this climb will be the most difficult physical challenge we will ever encounter. Even though at times we wanted to quit, all of us achieved the ascent. In the process, we uncovered the truth about how strong we are in body, mind, and spirit.

After reveling for a while on top, we descend the other side of the mountain toward our campground for the night, passing mountain goats along the way. I make sure to give the riders heading up a thumbs-up, hoping that my encouragement can make a difference for them as it had for me.

Tonight we are staying at a tacky, Roman-themed campground. We dine on site, too tired to ride to town. Near the restaurant is a karaoke bar, and as we eat, we listen to French singers attempt to sing English-language songs. They massacre the Village People, Queen, and U2. A Frenchman singing "YMCA" is the worst and funniest karaoke I've ever heard. (I'm sure the French would find it equally amusing for Americans to attempt to sing their songs.)

My tent is a quarter mile from the bathroom, and I had to put it on gravel. Despite the inconveniences, I sleep deeply and peacefully, satisfied that I conquered this giant mountain—with a hangover—and survived.

Photo by Eric Ben Attar.
Nearing the top of a wicked climb up Mont Ventoux.

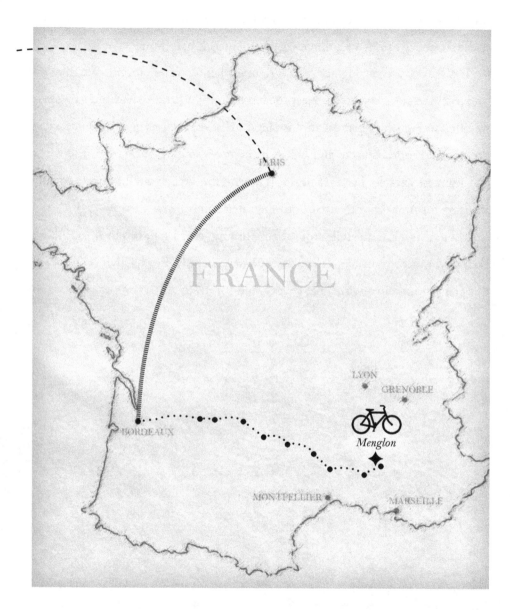

ROUTE NOTES: *Cycle from Vaison-la-Romaine to Menglon. Travel through the olive town of Nyons. Climb through most of the ride with a final ascent up Col de Prémol.*

DISTANCE: *65 miles or 105 kilometers*

Chapter 20

A DAY IN
OLIVE COUNTRY

L e Tour de France est dans les Pyrénées!" shouts one of the construction workers as I ride by.

The rest of the construction crew laughs. They think I should be riding in the mountains with the Tour de France riders instead of in the valleys of Provence. Spandex-clad, middle-aged women on bikes are obviously not an everyday occurrence in Nyons (pronounced "nee-ON").

After my climb up Mont Ventoux, I thought meandering through the villages would be the perfect day-after ride. Nyons, my first stop, is known as the olive capital of France. But the area is not just blessed with the gnarled trunks and silvery leaves of the olive tree. Nyons' temperate climate and rich soil encourage a bounty. Fruit trees hang heavily with cherries, nectarines, and apricots. Blue lavender, basil, and thyme grow wild in the hot summer sun. And of course, as in all of France, vineyards stretch across the land.

The latitude of Nyons is similar to my hometown in Montana. Why is southern France blessed with orchards of fruit and olives while south central Montana is covered with brown prairie grass? The Mediterranean Sea makes the difference, giving Nyons a microclimate where palm trees sway in the wind. In contrast, Montana has a steppe climate, more like the interior lands of Russia, China, or Mongolia.

Provence spans the northern edge of the Sahara, but it avoids desert extremes due to the Mediterranean Sea. When the hot desert air blows across the sea into Provence, the typical climate of six rainless months is reduced to three. Summer is the dry time of Provence, and the plants in the region have adapted to withstand the arid months. Winters are wet with moderate temperatures thanks to the balmy sea air.

My first stop in Nyons is a computer shop with Wi-Fi. Internet access had been nonexistent or expensive at the past two campgrounds, and I still haven't heard an update on the cat. In my last email, I encouraged Alex to email all the missing pet hotlines. Finally, I receive a message from Alex, but the news isn't good.

"I called all of those numbers and left messages because no one answered. I'm going to the shelter to see if they found him today, and I'm going to put in a report and a picture of him."

Oreo has been missing more than a week, and I'm not hopeful he'll return. A part of me feels upset that I'm not there to help find him. I feel so useless checking my email in France. All I can offer Alex now is my support to let her know that I recognize that she's doing everything she can.

It's noon by the time I finish writing a return email to Alex. I decide since I'm in Nyons, known for its olives, I should stop by the olive museum. Every shop, including the museum, will be shut down until two. (Siestas aren't just for Spain.) So I find an open-air restaurant and order the special—a ham salad (yes, the French love ham even on their salads) with tomatoes, cheese, and a thick olive oil dressing. The dressing is made with Nyons olives and the flavor is rich and mellow. I have some time, and so I also order rosé wine, refreshing and light on a hot, dry day.

After lunch, I ride to the Musée de l'Olivier (Museum of the Olive Tree). The museum doesn't open until 2:45, and I wait a half hour in the blistering hot sun. Promptly at the appointed hour, a car pulls up and out walks a man with a purposeful stride. He must be in his eighties, with his prune-like skin and snow-white hair.

"Bonjour," he says and asks for my four-euro entrance fee.

The man introduces himself as René. He doesn't speak English, but he gives me an English version of the museum guide. I walk around, looking at the old presses, jars, and photographs depicting the olive industry's history in France. The first olive tree was planted in Provence more than 10,000 years ago.

As I walk through the museum, I wonder: If the French olive oil is so great, why haven't I heard of it before? I pose my question in French to René.

"Is Italian olive oil better than French olive oil?"

He shakes his head slowly in response as if to say, "I can't believe you'd ask such a stupid question."

"C'est très compliqué." Maybe too complex for the dim-witted American.

René gathers the visitors in the museum so he can explain everything he knows about olive oil in encyclopedia-like detail. Olive oil is grown in regions within certain climate zones. Production stretches throughout France, Italy, Spain, and even in California. Much like it does for wine, the land determines the taste of the oil.

He doesn't criticize the Italian oil, but he disdains Spanish oil.

"C'est amère," he says while puckering his lips.

Amère? I tell him I don't know that word. René asks for help from the other visitors.

"It means bitter," a man says in a French accent.

René claims French oil is some of the best in the world. All of Nyons oil is certified by the Institut National de l'Appellation d'Origine (INAO). The INAO is the same board that calls a Bordeaux wine a Bordeaux. The INAO not only looks at the region where the olive (or grape) is grown, it also measures the levels of certain elements contained within the oil. To be called a Nyons olive oil, it must have a specified level of lipids, vitamins, and other specific qualities.

As René's lecture continues, I find myself challenged trying to understand since the words he uses are precisely related to olive oil. A pair of travelers—the Frenchman, who helped me earlier and a Dutchman who towers over me—serve as my translators. After explaining something, René asks me if I understand. Sometimes I decipher part of what he says but not all. The Frenchman tries to explain, and the Dutchman fills in the blanks. This takes a long time, and after an hour and fifteen minutes, I have no time to spare. At 4:00 p.m. I tell René and the group I have to leave.

René seems disappointed.

"Où allez-vous?" he asks, wondering where I'm going.

"Un moment," I reply and go outside to retrieve the day's route map and show him my next stop at Menglon.

He looks at the map, unconvinced that leaving is the best course for me. He had asked me earlier if I was single, and now he has a plan.

"Restez. Il pense vous êtes charmante," he says this as he motions to the tall, chunky Dutchman.

The Dutchman looks downward but gives a bashful smile. I don't care how charming the Dutchman finds me; I'm not equally charmed. And I have fifty miles to ride.

"Je suis désolée, mais je dois partir."

In France, the word for "sorry" literally translates to "desolate." So I'm expressing extreme sorrow and discontent when I say this. French is so polite. I bid farewell to René, the beefy Dutchman, and the rest of the group, and I hop on my bicycle toward Menglon.

Based on the distance to camp, my ride should take two-and-a-half to three hours—even going slowly. I didn't expect the sizzling heat and the climb of 2,300 feet (701 meters) up a mountain. My legs are already trashed from tackling Mont Ventoux yesterday.

I travel on remote alpine roads where the scenery changes from lush, fertile valley to forests and rivers. Not many villages lie on mountaintops, and so the trip is lonely and isolated with few water stops since there are no bars or cafés around to fill up my bottle.

The route seems endless, and as I near camp I realize my ride has taken four hours from the time I left Nyons. Not only have the climb and hot temperatures taken their toll, I'm also out of energy since I only had a protein bar after my lunchtime salad. After entering Menglon, I ride a mile down a hill in search of the campground. When I don't see any signs, I ride back uphill to town. I see a chocolate-skinned girl who looks about ten.

"Parlez-vous anglais?" I hope she speaks English because I don't see anyone else in this sleepy village.

"No, I don't speak English," she says in English, then switches to French. *"Attendez!"*

I wait as instructed, while the girl sprints down the street. She enters a house two blocks away. Soon, she walks out of the house with a woman who looks to be my age. I ride my bicycle toward them.

The woman speaks in perfect English with an American accent. She tells me to find the camp, I'll have to go down the road I had traveled on and ride beyond concrete mixers. How could I have ever understood that in French? And why is this American woman living in Menglon, an isolated mountain town? I leave without asking. I'm too tired to be inquisitive, and I don't want to try to find the campground in the dark.

I arrive at camp at eight, late for dinner. Skipping my shower, I change clothes and meet the group at the campground restaurant in my disheveled state. I'm crabby because the directions to camp weren't clear, but my annoyance fades when my cycling buddies probe my day.

"How was the museum?" asks David.

"How did you know about that?"

"Beth told us."

I had forgotten that Beth had seen me in Nyons, and I had told her my plans to visit the museum. They laugh as I recount the tale of my rejected Dutch boyfriend.

"Nancy, you never know," says Ian. "You may have had something in common with the chap."

"Yeah, right. He looked like he hasn't ridden a bike since boyhood. He never would have made it up Ventoux."

"There's more to romance than biking," says Ian.

I know Ian is right, not necessarily about the Dutchman, but about romance in general. Maybe having such high standards has been part of my problem. Really, how many single cyclists over forty even live in Billings? Maybe a handful? And is being a cyclist more important than being someone with a kind heart and passion for life?

A friend of mine is married to a man who she affectionately describes as looking like a troll. She claims his looks don't matter to her: "It's not the package but what's on the inside."

It wouldn't be so easy for me to have a troll next to me in bed. Every once in a while, I can overlook someone's appearance for a time, but eventually I can't take it. I've tried to tell myself that a man's hairy back, fat belly, or small hands shouldn't matter. But it does. I could never date a man who looked like a troll, a hobbit, or any fantasy character.

"I wish I could be more accepting," I say to Ian.

"You can be," he says. "You just have to work at it."

$\mathscr{I}$F THE SHOE FITS...

by Nancy Sathre-Vogel, world cycling adventurist

- **Cleats** – Many cyclists find they are more comfortable pedaling in dedicated, hard-soled cycling shoes. These are designed with rigid soles to transfer energy to the pedals more efficiently and cleats to hold your feet firmly on the pedals. That efficiency and comfort comes at a price. Due to the stiffness of the sole, they are not easy to walk in. You may also find that you must replace cleats more often on a tour due to the wear and tear of walking. You'll want to carry walking shoes for longer excursions.

- **Mountain biking shoes** – If you don't want to wear stiff-soled cycling shoes, mountain biking shoes may work for you. They have a more flexible sole that is still stiff enough to be reasonably efficient. Mountain bike shoes are great for the tourist because they are reasonably efficient and their recessed cleats make it much more comfortable for walking than stiff-soled cycling shoes. Some people, however, prefer to carry regular shoes for long walks, hiking, or extensive sightseeing trips.

- **Regular sneakers** – Some cyclists want the simplicity of cycling in regular shoes. If you choose the low-tech option, you'll need to consider how you will keep your feet on your pedals. You may use toe clips, Power Grips, or spiky pedals to hold your feet in place.

Connect with Nancy at www.familyonbikes.org.

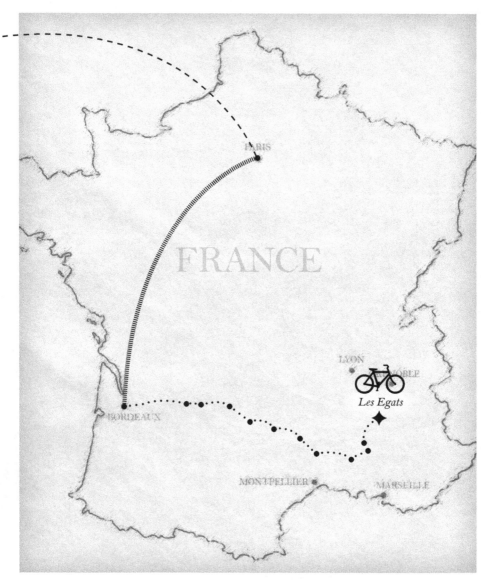

ROUTE NOTES: *Cycle from Menglon to Les Egats. We will tackle some hefty climbs with the highest being the Col de Menée at 4,560 feet (1,402 meters). Tonight's meal will highlight a local specialty called tartiflette, a creamy, cheesy potato dish.*

DISTANCE: *48 miles or 77 kilometers*

Chapter 21

CLIMBING THE COLS

"Y*odel-lady-hoooooooo*," I bellow out.

When I wrote Alex that I would be riding in the French Alps, she had a request: "Yodel for me." Why not? I'm by myself on an out-of-the-way road.

I laugh out loud at myself as I slowly ride up the small mountain road through the Prealps. This is a different France: a wild, rocky, secluded place. Lavender, poppies, and other wildflowers blossom in meadows warmed by the alpine sun. Tiny villages occasionally appear with stucco and stone houses lined with gardens. Instead of mountain flowers, the gardens bloom with roses in shades from pale peach to scarlet red. I breathe in the fragrant, fresh smell of flowers, mountain air, and grassy meadows, stopping frequently to take photos.

After staring out with the group this morning, once again I am riding on my own. This time it's not because I'm riding faster than everyone. Today, my pace is slower as I meander my way up, enjoying the scenery. I want to take it easy because tomorrow is our big ascent up Alpe d'Huez, another famed Tour de France climb.

My journey across France has taught me to embrace my time alone. I've learned to travel at my own pace, stop when I want, and stay in a place as long as I desire. Being on my own has proven more refreshing than trying to fit in with other people.

Why haven't I discovered this in my personal life? I'm always molding myself to make things work with the latest man. When a man I date doesn't fit me quite right, I become a chameleon, changing my colors to adapt to him.

"You need to find someone who fits you," Kathleen has told me repeatedly.

I never really got it until now while traveling on my own through France. Why act like someone I'm not? It will just lead to frustration and resentment in the long run. It's better to be alone and myself. At least, that's what I'm discovering on my journey.

It's not just women who do this. Some of the men I've dated share this chameleon quality. When they tried to adapt to fit me, I wanted to run. Three non-cycling men offered to buy bikes so they could ride with me. One of the men, Bob, told me that he had been sedentary for a decade but I had inspired him to start riding. Bob found a bargain bike on eBay—some steel bike with a brand name that I didn't recognize. Just in case the bike didn't impress me enough, he tried to lure me in with our picture-perfect future. We could move somewhere together where we could ride our bikes year-round. We would live near vineyards, maybe the pinot noir region of Oregon. I was flattered by his attention at first, but the onslaught became excruciating. I told him that all of the talk was wearing me out. Eventually, I gave him the e-dump.

It's easy to make fun of someone who obviously tries too hard. But what about me? Haven't I been as guilty as Bob in some of my relationships? Perhaps it's less obvious when you do it yourself. I wasn't so overt as to take up cycling to impress someone, but still, I gave myself up in subtle ways. I once went to the theater to watch a sci-fi movie at midnight with my then boyfriend. Why? I don't like the genre and can't keep my eyes open past ten. I kept seeing Jim even though he admitted cheating on me. And Dante—why was I wasting my time on a man who bluntly told me he doesn't want a relationship with me? Riding across France alone has shown me that I don't need to mold myself to fit anyone. I hope I can remember when I return home.

For now, I have Col de Menée to ride up. The mountain pass climbs more than seven miles at a 4 percent grade, but after tackling Mont Ventoux, Menée seems simple. At the top is a tunnel cut through the mountain. This is the worst part of the climb. I enter the darkness and hear the rumble of an engine behind me. Without lights on my bicycle, I worry that the car will smack me. I pedal faster. As I exit, I see Drew in the support van behind me. Maybe it's a coincidence, but I like to think he followed me to make sure I made it out safely.

I take my time on the descent. At the bottom of the col I spot the others at a café in the valley. It's a gorgeous setting with Mont Aiguille rising in the background and flowers blossoming in the foreground. A swimming pool near the café tempts me.

"It would feel so great to jump in," I say to Nate, who is sitting beside me at the table.

Nate doesn't reply. Instead he strips off his jersey, bike shoes and socks, and plunges into the pool with only his biking shorts. I laugh at his free-spirited leap. Maybe Nate is just being himself, too. My initial view and subsequent dismissal of him changes in that instant. I admire his uncompromising nature. I could learn from Nate.

After lunch I join David and Kate, who are riding slowly up the next climb, Col Accarias. Kate had ridden in the van to the lunch site, but I have to give her credit for at least trying some of the climbs this afternoon. This must be a sacrifice for Kate, who seems to prefer a leisurely day shopping with the crew for afternoon snacks and breakfast. I wonder what motivated her to get out and ride today. Maybe she's being a chameleon.

Col Accarias is a relatively easy climb compared to the ascents this morning. While David and I ride ahead and converse, Kate struggles behind us, breathing heavily and slowly grinding her legs.

We wait for Kate at the top of the col. When she arrives we take pictures of each other by the sign marking the summit of Col Accarias. Despite her struggle, Kate seems happy. She smiles big for the camera, her arm around her husband. Her face glistens with sweat. She looks beautiful— and satisfied.

I leave them after the climb and continue on my own, catching up with some of the other riders. Despite my intent to go slowly, I pick up the pace as I near camp, like a horse wanting its oats after a long ride. One last three-mile climb remains before camp. I catch myself pushing too hard, and I ease up to save my legs for the next day's challenge. Several of the riders start a hammerfest, what cyclists call pushing themselves to the limit on a ride. I don't rise to the bait, sticking with my moderate tempo.

The campground tonight is such a treat: showers with curtains, sinks with soap, even a clothesline—and no open-air urinals. Better still is tonight's dinner. The campground owners cook us *tartiflette*—think au gratin potatoes with ham. But that doesn't describe the rich, smooth, tangy taste and comfort of the *tartiflette*. The secret? Reblochon cheese is sliced over the top before the dish is baked. This isn't your ordinary supermarket block cheese. Reblochon is cheese perfection, made in the region using unpasteurized milk from French cows that graze in alpine meadows.

It's so good, I can't stop eating. I down my 5,000 calories of *tartiflette* with rosé wine. As I go back for dessert, Simon looks me over.

"Are you drunk?" he says. I hate his snide comments.

"No, I'm not drunk."

I've eaten so much that I don't think it's possible for the wine to soak through all the food. My stomach aches by the time I've finished eating. No worries. It will be good fuel for tomorrow's ride up Alpe d'Huez.

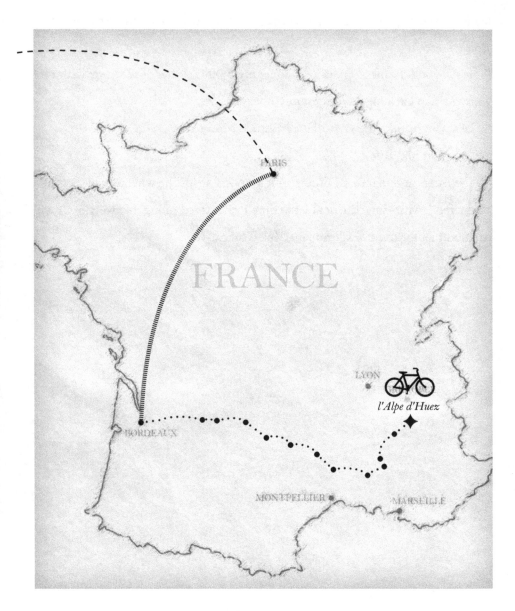

ROUTE NOTES: *Cycle from Les Egats to l'Alpe d'Huez. This is the final day of riding. We'll end up at the top of the famous Tour de France climb. In French, the mountain's full name means: The Alp of the town of Huez.*

DISTANCE: *32 miles or 51 kilometers*

Chapter 22

THE LAST BIG CLIMB

D id you put your foot down when you rode up Ventoux?" asks
Simon at breakfast.

"Yes. Why does it matter?" I say.

"Then it doesn't count."

"What do you mean it doesn't count?"

"A proper cyclist wouldn't put a foot down during a climb. If you do, it doesn't count," Simon says in his snooty voice.

Yes, I had put my foot down, more than once, while climbing Mont Ventoux. Who was Simon to say that it didn't count? He skipped riding up Ventoux and joined Kate on the alternative, easier ride to Châteauneuf du Pape where they met his parents and sister for his gourmet birthday lunch and wine.

After breakfast, I pack my tent. *Not a proper cyclist.* Screw him. And who says "proper" anyway? At least I made it up Ventoux—more than he could say.

I squeeze the air out of the sleeping pad with more force than usual. I tightly fold my sleeping bag into a roll. I jam these into my suitcase. I'll show him. I won't stop this time. As my resolve kicks in, my anger dissipates. A new emotion emerges: sadness. Last night was my final night of camping. Today will be my last ride. Tomorrow our tour will be over.

I've traveled so far in two weeks. Yes, I've cycled across France, but more importantly, I've journeyed inside myself and rediscovered the girl who relaxes in the world. I've let go of all the structure and obligations, learning how to just be with myself. I've grown to love the people and the places that I visit each day. I'll miss so many things—practicing my French, eating pain au chocolat, taking photos of the countryside and people, and exploring quaint villages. I'm leaving it all behind. Soon, I'll return to my home in Montana's prairie land, my work in the corporate world, and familiar people and places. I hope I can find a way to take a bit of France back with me.

Today, a challenging but short ride awaits. We have two climbs: Col d'Ornon and Alpe d'Huez. My focus will be riding—not dawdling to take photos along the way. I don't plan on being impressed with the scenery of the Alps. After all, Montana is a state with mountain ranges galore.

My plans change as the Alps unfold before me. I'm astonished by how close the mountains seem. The ranges shoot straight up from the valley below rather than gradually building, like the Rockies. Instead of rough terrain, hearty pines, and aspens, the Alps are covered with green mountain meadows and wildflowers. Despite my intention of racing up the mountain, I slow down and stop when I see a field of poppies. I set my bike on the ground, scale down the hill, and snap a photo of the poppies with the high mountain peak in the background. Crouching on the ground, I shoot the flowers close up.

Why do I appreciate the beautiful scenery so much in France? Montana is an equally magnificent place with high peaks, wildflowers, and nature at my back door. I would never think of bringing a camera on a bike ride and snapping photos. Have I really become so unappreciative? Maybe I can bring France back with me by changing how I see my everyday world.

My Aussie friend, Robbie, also stops to take pictures. I ride with him as we continue to climb toward the summit of Col d'Ornon.

"Did you hear Simon say that it doesn't count to climb a mountain if you put your foot down?" I ask him.

"Don't listen to him, Nance. Of course it counts! That was one tough climb. I didn't think I was going to make it. And if you need to stop this time, then stop."

"I hope I won't need to."

"It doesn't matter if you do. It's not a race."

Our conversation stops as the road becomes more vertical. This is harder than I expected. Yet the steep part only lasts three miles. I should be fine for Alpe d'Huez.

At the top of Col d'Ornon we meet our group at a bar. We sit outside in the crisp mountain air, basking in the sun that seems more intense at this elevation. Some of my biking pals relax in reclining chairs. I notice again how jocular the riders are with each other. I feel like the kid at school who doesn't have a best friend but to whom people are still nice anyway. Being an outsider doesn't bother me too much anymore. Having made the choice early on to soak in the French countryside and people, I've experienced everything I desired for my Tour de France. Yet, I can see that the other cyclists made an equally good choice in forging a bond through their shared experiences. We take our last group photo, and then head toward our final ascent.

While Mont Ventoux had scared me, I'm relaxed about climbing Alpe d'Huez. I know that the first few miles of the climb will be steep. After that, it levels out and a rider can recover on the twenty-one hairpin turns. Still, the climb is eight-and-a-half-miles with an average grade of 7.9 percent. But after riding Ventoux with a hangover, this will be easy.

I'm worried about Kate making the climb. David hadn't pressured her to bike over the past two weeks, but he insisted that she ride up Alpe d'Huez. To me it seems like a bad idea with her lack of cycling experience.

The first part of the climb challenges me, and I immediately shift into granny mode. Surprisingly, my body adjusts quickly to the rhythm of climbing. I don't feel like I'm going to die like I had at the start of Mont Ventoux. This is progress. I'm not riding fast, but I am riding steady.

A mile or so into the climb, I pass Kate, who started before me. She's doing surprisingly well for not having ridden much during the past two weeks.

"Allez! Allez! Allez!" I say to her. "Looking good."

I start off strong, and then I start tiring. The combination of more than 700 miles of riding and climbing mountains has chipped away at my fortitude. Nate whizzes by me. He's looking powerful. Then Keith and Jenny pass me by. She's riding faster than I expected. She's breathing hard as she pumps uphill. I just don't have the drive to try to catch her; let her conquer the mountain. As Robbie told me, it's not a race. My only goal is to get to the top without stopping.

Alpe d'Huez is frequently a stage of the Tour de France. The Tour riders will be climbing this very mountain in four days. The road is quite busy with traffic—much busier than Mont Ventoux had been. The atmosphere seems hectic compared to Ventoux's pristine environment.

Spectators have parked their RVs along the road, jockeying for a prime view of the Tour de France riders. The RVers seem ready to party, like tailgaters at an American football game. They sit outside their campers with drinks in hand, talking loudly while the thumping music blares from loud speakers. They casually watch the recreational cyclists pass by. While I heard encouraging shouts of *"Allez"* as I rode up Ventoux, there's no support from the rowdy spectators on this mountain. One woman near an RV tells me to "quit." At least I think that's what she said. She has a thick Dutch accent. Maybe she said "quick"—but I'm riding so slow that I can't imagine she'd use that word.

I'm not going to quit, and I'm not going to quicken my pace. Today, I'll ride steady up the mountain and keep my foot off the ground.

The hairpin turns provide some flat spots of relief from the climb. The roads through the alpine villages also level out, which eases the toll on my legs. This ascent is challenging—but not like Mont Ventoux. Or maybe my more relaxed attitude makes the climb seem easier.

A commercial photographer standing on the shoulder of the road takes my photo with two miles left to ride. He's cheerful, asking me where I'm from. He perks me up for my final two-mile climb to the top. And I still haven't put my foot down.

As I near the top, a village emerges. L'Alpe d'Huez is a famous ski resort. There are shops, people, and cars everywhere. I'm just another of the countless cyclists riding up the mountain. Making it to the top feels anticlimactic. I see my fellow cyclists sitting outside at a café. They give me a lackluster cheer but no claps or hugs.

"The finish line is twenty feet away," Ellie says.

I cross the finish line, even though it doesn't really matter, and I circle back to join the group. I have met my goal and can make the claim of being a "proper" Alpe d'Huez cyclist. I finished in an hour and twenty-two minutes. The climb took me more than twice as long to finish as course record-holder Marco Pantani, who finished in thirty-six minutes and fifty seconds.

Simon sits at the table, but he never asks if I put my foot down, and it's not important for me to mention it to him. Jenny talks about how well she rode up the mountain. I congratulate her. Nate is thrilled that he finished the ride in under an hour, beating everyone else in our group. He asks me to take his photo on the podium where the top three Tour de France finishers will pose in a few days. I'm happy for him, but the photo will have to wait. I'm more interested in watching Kate complete her mountain challenge. David finished well before me, and now he has turned around to ride the last few miles with Kate. As they near the bar, I stand up and cheer her accomplishment. She really did it!

"Allez! Allez! Allez!"

Kate tells me that her ride was challenging, and she took a few rest stops to make it through. I wouldn't dream of telling her that the climb didn't count because she put her foot down. She's elated that she finished, and her husband is proud of her accomplishment. I see now that I was wrong to be so judgmental of her and her husband. Kate was just doing her own thing. Why should I care if she didn't want to ride? And David wasn't pushing her to be someone that she's not. He has been encouraging her to find the strength within by moving beyond her comfort zone.

Before we leave, I snap a photo of Nate on the podium. He stands with his chest puffed, looking out in the distance. He seems so proud of his accomplishment, almost like he really did win the stage at the Tour de France.

There's no tent to set up after the ride. Instead, I'll sleep in a hotel, and as the only single female customer, I have a room to myself. What a luxury after camping for two weeks. There's a bathroom with towels, soap, and shampoo; a real bed with sheets; even a blow dryer.

I can't resist soaking in the tub, and I relax for more than an hour. After my bath, I press my silk skirt and black shirt. The last time I wore the skirt I had been out with Dante on my last night in Montreal. I haven't heard from him since the text message two weeks ago, but it doesn't matter. I need to get over him, push away these thoughts, and enjoy myself at our last dinner.

Before I join the group, I check my email. I can't believe what I see: a message from Dante.

"*Allez, Allez, Allez!* If you're reading this from the Big Sky State, welcome home too!"

Disregarding my intent to be done with him, I reply immediately. I write briefly about my bike travels and then add something more personal.

"I actually was thinking of you tonight. I had on my flowered silk skirt, and the last time I wore it was the last time I saw you. PS: Maybe you should meet me in Paris."

As I write this, I know that I've gone into my fantasy zone. He's in Vermont, and I seriously doubt that he would fly to Paris. I'm back to being the romance novel heroine.

With all the time I took on primping and writing the email, I'm the last one to arrive to meet the group. Everyone is relaxing with drinks on an outside deck. Simon spots me first.

"Nancy is looking hot," he says.

I do look pretty good. Especially if you've only seen me in cycling wear for the past two weeks.

I smile and exaggerate a hip-swinging walk. Ian reclines in a chair, and I saunter over to him, sit on his lap, and snuggle next to him on the chair. Then I smile and gave him a big kiss on the cheek. He turns bright red. Everyone else laughs as Ellie takes a photo.

After dinner, some of the group heads out to the town disco. I rush back to my room. I can't wait to check my email. There's another one from Dante.

Regarding Paris on Sunday: Sounds delectable! See you there! (Sunday in September, right?) I know a great little bar on the corner of Boulevard Saint-Michel and Boulevard Saint-Germain on the Left Bank. Be there or risk seeing the pizza guy on Tuesdays of each week of the month and being fed his war stories about the bachelor set and laundry.

He wasn't serious, I'm sure. But what if he was? He's a doctor. He could afford a last-minute ticket if he wanted one.

My reply is instantaneous. "Not September. Tomorrow!"

I want to wait up to see if he will reply, but the soft bed calls me. I rest peacefully. The ride is behind me and in my fantasy thinking, a new relationship with Dante is ahead.

Poppies in the Alps.

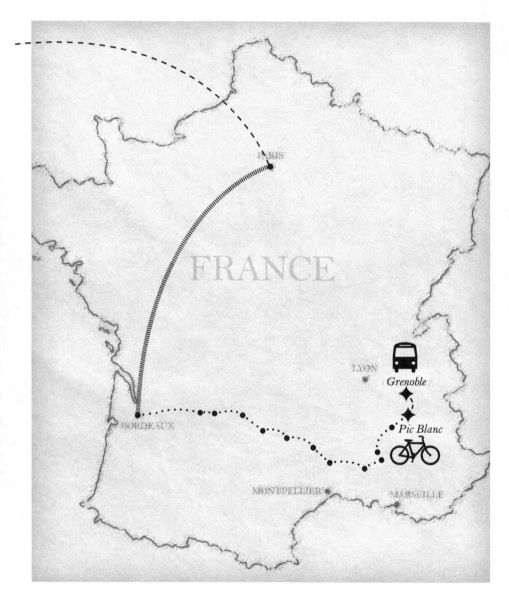

ROUTE NOTES: *Ride the gondola from Alpe d'Huez to Pic Blanc with spectacular view of 20 percent of France. Take bus from Alpe d'Huez to Grenoble.*

DISTANCE: *40 miles or 64 kilometers by bus*

Chapter 23

ON TOP OF THE WORLD

I slept soundly last night, but I've awakened before eight, ready for breakfast, as has been my habit over the past two weeks. Even though I'm starving, my first priority is email. There's a message waiting:

"Too bad I'll have to take a rain check on Paris this Sunday—I will be in Montreal."

Heavy sigh. Not that I really expected he'd meet me in Paris, but my heart hoped he would.

Several of my riding companions are downstairs at breakfast. David, Robbie, Simon, and I decide to take the gondola to the top of the mountain. Ian says he'll tag along for a walk through the village.

We have a problem: we don't know where to find the gondola. Simon says he'll ask for directions. This seems to make sense: he certainly speaks French more fluently than I do. Ian, however, has a different idea.

"These French people don't want to help an arrogant Englishman asking for directions," he says. "Let the charming American ask instead."

"You mean me?" I say.

"Yes, you ask for directions, Nancy. They'll want to help you."

I stifle my laugh. Simon doesn't say a word.

I ask for directions and we find our way to the gondola. Three cyclists with mountain bikes share our car on the first leg of the journey. The ski runs serve as downhill mountain bike trails in summer. The cyclists will ride down the steep trails back to the starting point. When we get to the top, we watch them descend. It looks treacherous to me.

At the first stop we switch gondolas for our final ascent to the top of the mountain. We reach Pic Blanc (White Peak) after a half-hour gondola ride. When we exit, we are chilled by the cool air at 10,826 feet (3,300 meters).

I had considered the views atop Mont Ventoux as panoramic, but they pale in comparison. Ventoux was a plasma television while Pic Blanc is an IMAX movie screen. We're high above the world and see mountaintops hundreds of miles away. A brochure says that from the top of Pic Blanc, one can see 20 percent of France. There's a telescope on the top, and I look through it to see the white, rocky top of Mont Ventoux.

While the air is cool, the sun warms us. We walk around and use such trite adjectives as "amazing," "beautiful," and "spectacular." Words fail to capture the majesty of the view from the top. For me, it's a special moment. I've ridden across France—through the vineyards, river valleys, lush fields of Provence, the cols, and the Alps. Now I'm on top of the world. That's how I feel about the views and the journey.

After our visit to Pic Blanc, it's time to wish four of our comrades farewell. Robbie, Ian, Simon, and Nate will stay on with the Wide Open Road tour group and spend time riding in the Alps and watching the Tour de France. With quick hugs and goodbye waves, they ride off to meet the crew for their next adventure.

The two couples and I catch a bus to Grenoble for travel the next day. I take out my camera on the way down Alpe d'Huez to capture photos of the steep, twisting roads that we climbed up yesterday. I move across the aisle of the bus to catch the first hairpin turn. As I'm clicking away, I hear my water bottle fall off my seat and roll forward. The man sitting in front of me picks it up. He's rugged, lean, and tanned. Obviously, he spends a lot of time outdoors. I'd say he's handsome, except for his weird hair—a buzz cut with hair in front that's rolled up like a sausage.

"Great. That's what I want," he says in English with a French accent.

I move back to my seat.

"Can I have my water bottle?" I ask.

"No. I'm going to keep it as a souvenir," he says in a firm voice.

"Please? Can I have it?"

"No. I want it."

I really do want my water bottle back, but I'm getting nowhere with this conversation. I'm starting to feel sick from the bus ride as the driver swerves around the hairpins.

"I really need it—*pour mon vélo,*" I say.

"Too bad. It's mine now."

I don't answer. Then he speaks again.

"Would you autograph it for me?"

Seeing my opportunity I say, "Yes!"

"No, forget it. You won't give it back."

Finally, he smiles and says, "I'll give you your water bottle back."

We introduce ourselves. His name is Pierre. He talks to me for a while and includes David in the conversation. Pierre tells us that he had been at Alpe d'Huez doing some military training. Originally Swiss, he's now a French citizen and is in the French ski patrol in intelligence. He was formerly part of the French Foreign Legion. (This is starting to sound made up now, I realize, but that's what he's saying.)

Pierre and I talk about the people in France. He thought they were rude and snobbish. I tell him my experience sharply contradicted his.

"That's because you are so gorgeous," he says. "Who wouldn't want to talk to you?"

I smile—caught a little off-guard by his compliment. Who would think that someone would flirt with me on a bus?

He asks me where I'm from and where I work. It seems unusual for a stranger to probe about such detailed personal information, especially someone who claims to work in intelligence, so I keep my answers nonspecific.

"Can I have your email address?" he asks.

"Why don't you give me yours?"

He writes it down on a piece of paper. I don't intend to write him back. I'll admit that the idea of a chance encounter with a stranger perks up my romantic side. Still, even if he had been Mr. Perfect, it's time for me to learn to appreciate myself instead of waiting for someone else to validate me.

We arrive in Grenoble in less than an hour. We say *au revoir* to Pierre, who is catching the train to Geneva. David tells me that he thinks Pierre has "taken a fancy" to me. His British colloquialism makes me laugh.

The five of us head toward the hotel, this one even shabbier than the one in Bordeaux. We dine together at an Italian restaurant and are back to cordial conversations, the same as we had the first night the group met. With dinner completed, we head back to the hotel and give each other goodbye hugs before retiring to our rooms. David and Kate will leave early in the morning so this will be the last time I see them. Keith and Jenny said they'd help me cart my luggage to the train depot tomorrow morning.

My room in the hotel is unbearably hot. There's no air conditioning, and so I open my window and breathe in the stale city air. All night, the noises wake me. People party outside my window, and trains from the nearby depot screech at regular intervals. I had tired of camping, but that was heaven compared to this stifling hot room. I miss the fresh air, chirping birds, and the snoring of my neighbors.

But there's no going back. I'm off to my final stop in France: Paris.

SAVE MONEY ON PARIS MUSEUMS

*by Matt Scott, French travel guide/review
writer and tour guide*

- **Museum Pass** – If you're staying in the city for a few days, a Museum Pass is essential. It allows you not only to skip the queues in practically all of the city's museums but also to access many of the major monuments as well—such as the towers of Notre Dame and the Arc de Triomphe. *www.parismuseumpass.com*

- **Free days** – All national museums are free on the first Sunday of each month (expect long queues), and if you're under twenty-five you can enter the Louvre for free every Friday night (after 6:00 p.m.). Many other museums offer free entry at various times. Check out Web sites of individual museums in advance.

- **Always free** – There are over a dozen free museums which are well worth checking out. Here are some examples:

o Le Petit Palais – Fine Arts Museum: *www.petitpalais.paris.fr*

o Musée Carnavalet – Museum of Paris History: *www.carnavalet.paris.fr*

o Modern Art Museum of Paris – *www.paris.org/Musees/Art.Moderne.Ville*

o The House of Victor Hugo – *www.musee-hugo.paris.fr*

- **Getting there** – Your first choice is to be like Parisians and walk to your destination. If you're not in walking distance, the Metro is the way to go. You can buy single trip tickets, a packet of ten tickets, or passes that last one to five days. *www.ratp.info*

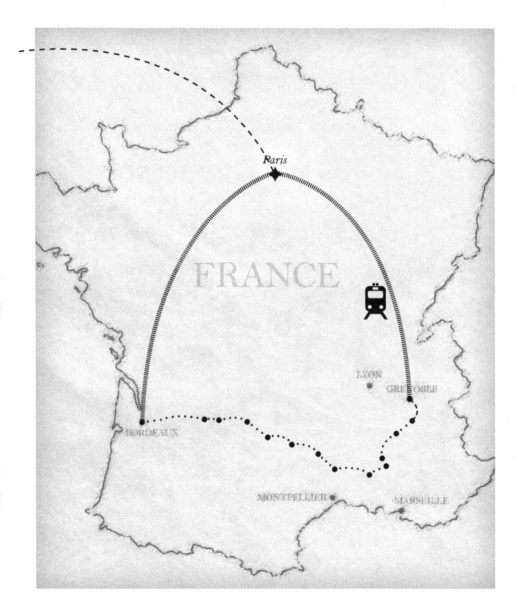

ROUTE NOTES: *Train from Grenoble to Paris. Spend three days exploring the City of Lights.*

DISTANCE: *398 miles or 640 kilometers*

Chapter 24

LAST STOP: PARIS

When I arrived in Paris for the first time, I hauled my luggage through the Charles de Gaulle Airport to find the train to Bordeaux. I never want to be a mule again, and I don't mind asking for help anymore. This time, Keith and Jenny assist in porting my luggage to the TGV station to catch my train out of Grenoble. Once I arrive in Paris, a former classmate of mine and his wife meet me at the depot. Who says I need to do everything by myself anyway?

I'm staying in Paris with Matt and Lynn. I know Matt from three years of evening MBA classes. He's a true-blue guy, an everyday superhero. He's never going to fly out of tall buildings, but he will rescue a damsel in distress with luggage and offer her a place to stay for a few days.

Matt is smart in all the ways I'm not. In class, he'd breeze through the answers to financial analysis and quantitative research problems before I even understood the question. He was the guy with the financial calculator who actually knew how to use it while I was amazed that such calculations even existed. Matt, an engineer, must be smart and thorough in his day job, too. He and his wife both worked for an oil company in Billings, and when their company offered them a chance to transfer to Paris, they jumped at it.

Once Matt and Lynn got settled, Matt sent another classmate and me an email inviting us to stay with him in Paris. Matt remembered that the two of us used to talk about visiting France. What a great opportunity—a place to stay near the Paris Opera and built-in American tour guides. He may have been surprised by my eager response to his invitation but he's too nice to ever admit it.

We drop my luggage off at their apartment. There's no time to relax; Matt wants to start immediately on my tourist itinerary. We begin at the Paris Opera, walk to the Arc de Triomphe along the River Seine, and down the Avenue des Champs-Élysées. In a week, riders will parade down this street on their final leg of the Tour de France.

Lynn and I walk quickly to keep up with Matt's strides. I feel like strolling instead of speed-walking down the street because I'm fascinated by the Parisian street scene. I notice people ride the same gray commuter bikes rented from stations throughout the city. Men pedal with suits and ties, women with skirts and heels. I notice the café tables set up for theater seating. Everyone faces the street as they watch the people walk or ride by. Most women have on black, sexy sunglasses. One woman dons a lime green hat, matching sleeveless shirt, and accessorizes with a little white dog walking beside her. I hurriedly capture the street scenes with my camera without really connecting to anyone. Matt and Lynn slow down as I snap my random photos. They must think I'm a little crazy as I click away at unknown people doing ordinary things.

Our final destination for the evening is the Eiffel Tower and the place is chaos. Two lines lead to the tower. Visitors can take an elevator to the third level at the very top or walk up stairs to reach the second level. The elevator line coils back and forth and must be a half-mile or longer. The line to the stairs is shorter and the entrance fee less, so that is our choice. Still, we must wait in a zigzag queue that covers several hundred feet.

The Eiffel Tower seems to represent a melting pot of cultures. I hear many different languages spoken. The American tourists seem obvious with their brightly colored clothes and bulky bodies. They talk louder than everyone. Police walk through the crowds armed with pistols and military men dressed in fatigues carry automatic weapons slung from their shoulders. It's unnerving for me to see the display of force, definitely unlike the tranquil French countryside.

I shift my focus to a young couple standing in line. They lean into each other, her left arm wrapped around his neck. His face is turned toward her, inches away from her face. He seems to be whispering secrets into her ear, and she smiles sweetly as he does. They can't be more than twenty, and they seem fully in love. It's fresh, innocent, sticky-sweet love. I'd like to think that no matter what our age, we can be open enough to experience young love. Maybe there's a way for me to wring out the old automated responses and pour in fresh possibilities.

Finally, it's our turn to climb the 710 stairs to the second level of the tower. I start out climbing swiftly to keep up with Matt's loping legs. We both slow down to wait for Lynn, who seems content to take her time.

When we arrive at the second level, I'm stunned by how much of Paris I see. On the summit of Pic Blanc I viewed expansive vistas of the countryside of France. Now, from my vantage point on the Eiffel Tower, I see concrete structures of the cityscape stretching to eternity. What a contrast from rural France.

At last our tourist evening winds down, and it's time for dinner at a café with views of the tower. As dusk descends, the structure beams like a Christmas tree with its twinkling lights and stars. The waiter asks for our order in English.

"How did he know to speak to us in English?" I ask Matt.

"They just can tell if you're American."

"But we're not dressed like the other tourists I saw." We're all dressed casually in neutral tops and jeans.

"They just know," says Matt.

This doesn't seem to bother him. I don't like the thought that my American-ness stands out. Don't get me wrong, I love my country, and I have a great deal of pride in being American. Still, I don't want people to lump me in with all the big loud peacocks I saw today.

After pasta and wine, we walk back to Matt and Lynn's apartment. I know how Parisians avoid obesity. Everywhere they go, they walk or ride bicycles. Matt, not overweight to start, said he lost twenty pounds after moving to Paris. What a contrast to most places in America, where we drive even if our destination is a few blocks away.

My room in the apartment feels luxurious: a comfortable bed, my own bathroom, even a computer with Internet access. A cool breeze flutters through the open window on a warm Parisian night as I sit at the desk and write emails. I start with Alex, telling her about the Eiffel Tower and the scenes from the streets of Paris. I ask about the dogs and whether she's heard anything about the cat. At this point, I'm doubtful that Oreo will return.

My next email is to Dante and I write about my fear at the adjustment of being home. I'm worried that after experiencing the freedom to just be myself in France, the old roles will confine my spirit. The tone of my email to him is friendly rather than flirty. Even though I still care for him, I've moved away from my fantasy zone, beyond dreaming that he will jet off to Paris to meet me.

Why had I clung onto the belief that he would suddenly want a future with me when he didn't want a commitment with anyone? "I've been on my own so long, I don't know if I can ever give up my freedom," he once told me. I remember thinking this would be a lonely way to live. I felt sorry for him and what he was missing. I judged his stance as a character flaw.

But maybe my projections were not true. Couldn't his decision to be alone reflect a lifestyle choice rather than a personality defect? Maybe *I'm* the one missing out because I haven't found contentment with my single life. Instead of looking inside to understand why I feel so lacking without romance, I've distracted myself with the latest Mister-Almost-Right. Yet no one can be right if I'm not satisfied by myself.

I realize something else, too. Despite how much I care for Dante, I can see that I need to stop hanging on to him and start moving on in my life. I deserve better than a half-hearted romance.

My second day in Paris will be crammed full with visits to historical places and museums. I think our itinerary is too aggressive for one day, but Matt seems determined to cross all of these off my must-see-in-Paris list. Despite the hectic schedule, I'm grateful that Matt and Lynn have taken the day off to show me around. Our first stop is Notre Dame Cathedral, known in French as "Our Lady of Paris."

At the time the cathedral was built, most people were illiterate. So instead of using words, the stories of the Bible are told through its portals, paintings, and stained-glass windows. The construction of Notre Dame took over 180 years to complete, starting in 1163 and finishing around 1345.

Back in college, Notre Dame seemed so exotic and far away. Twenty-five years later, I'm finally standing in front of the ancient religious structure. Many tourists crowd around the building on this July day, but their busyness doesn't distract me from soaking in the majesty of the cathedral.

My poster from college comes to life when I see the west façade of the building. Entranced, I walk toward one of the three arched doorways, the Portal of Sainte Anne. Two thirteenth-century wooden doors with wrought-iron décor serve as entryways, although the doors are shut. Extending above the doors is an intricately-sculpted archway. In the center is the Virgin Mary holding Jesus. She is flanked by angels and royalty. Many other stories come to life through the ancient stone carvings.

As I take in the beauty of the portal I hear people talking and cameras clicking, and yet I experience stillness. For so many years, I longed to see Notre Dame and France, and now I'm here. I feel moved, not so much from the beauty of the place but for the appreciation for finally living this experience. In this age of immediate gratification, we've lost the satisfaction of delayed fulfillment. There's a gift in the waiting.

Believe me: I'm no more patient than anyone. I want it now! When I don't get what I covet, I protest loudly. The universe doesn't heed my impatient, childish stomping. Throw a temper tantrum if you want; it will be when it will be. The universe has its own timing.

I'm especially impatient with relationships. Everything always seems to start out nicely when I begin dating. And then the internal dialogue begins. Where is this going? Am I just wasting my time? Is this going to work or not? It's as if I'm pulling open a flower seed looking for blossoms and destroying it in the process. I must learn to be patient and let the seeds sprout on their own accord.

I wander on my own to the back of the building where I see the gargoyles. They're creepy little monsters peering over the building edge. Their eyes stare blankly into the Paris sky as their mouths hang agape. The gargoyles are more than decorative; they have a functional purpose of draining water from the roof.

While studying the gargoyles, I hear the familiar coo from the countryside. *Hoo hooooo hooooo. Hoo hooooo hooooo.* A plump bird with a gray head and pinkish breast is perched in a tree. Nearby I see a couple—American tourists, I guess, by their requisite bright tops, walking sandals, and cameras.

"Excuse me. Do you know what kind of bird that is?" I ask them, pointing to the tree.

"Why, that's a mourning dove," says the man.

Some religious traditions believe that animals come into our lives to reveal messages from the spirit world. And I'm struck: it's no coincidence that the universal symbol of peace has been serenading me each morning in France. The mourning dove has been a SIGN! It's time to leave behind my frantic pace and relax into peace and beauty in my everyday world.

Back at the apartment, I spend a quiet evening with Matt and Lynn. On a balcony filled with potted flowers, we talk and enjoy a simple meal of bread, cheese, and wine. It's a relaxing evening of conversation and shared laughter. I would so much enjoy staying in Paris a bit longer, but in two days I'll be home.

I'm already feeling a bit lost thinking about the transition. There will be no more lingering over *cafés au lait,* stopping in a village because I want to, taking photos of the landscape, meeting strangers and becoming friends, practicing my French and learning new words every day. My hectic life awaits with a demanding job, daily responsibilities, and trying to squeeze in time to ride my bike. I'll strive to keep the part of me I discovered in my France, but I fear that the daily grind will make me forget the lessons from the mourning dove.

On my third day in Paris I will be on my own. Lynn leaves me her cell phone to use in case I get lost. I thank her and chuckle to myself. I rode 786 miles across France without a phone; my map to each night's campground served as my only guide. Now here I am in the urban center of France with people on every street corner who speak English, and I have a phone in case I need directions. Still, I'm touched by her caring nature.

I intend to make the most of my last day in France. Matt has a list of four tourist sites for me to see today, but I'm not worried about trying to fit everything in. I'll see how I feel, take some time to relax at a café, and maybe meet some new people. Today, instead of looking like an American tourist, I want to feel Parisian. To blend in I need to dress the part: black shirt, jeans, and stylish sunglasses. I've got to get the expression right. There's something about the way they hold their lips. It's a bit of a pout. I practice in the mirror. Not great, but I'll try it anyway. I'll know if I'm successful if Parisians speak to me in French rather than English.

I spend my morning lingering over impressionist paintings at the Musée d'Orsay. While I love browsing through the museum, it's such a nice day that I decide to skip the other museums and spend my afternoon at the Rodin Sculpture Garden.

While the other Parisian art galleries seemed bustling and frenzied, the garden relaxes me. The bronze sculptures appear to grow out of the earth, like the trees, shrubs, and flowers that adorn the grounds. I decide to wind down under the leafy trees at the outdoor café. Sparrows flit about, hoping to capture some of the crumbs left behind from diners. I order in French a salad, baguette, and some rosé wine to enjoy as I soak in the natural setting.

The garden is located on more than seven acres of land surrounding the Musée Rodin, in what used to be the Hôtel Biron. When he was alive, Rodin rented rooms in the hotel for art storage and eventually used them as a studio. He entertained his friends here in the untamed gardens surrounding the museum.

This quiet contemplation of art and nature is exactly what I need today. My routine is to stroll to a sculpture and then walk around it, seeing it from every angle. Every few sculptures I sit on a nearby bench to feel the art around me.

I smile as I watch a boy who sits near *The Thinker*, attempting to mimic the contemplative pose. I also notice several people sketching the statues. It's been since college when I last have drawn or painted. Several years ago I did try to incorporate art into my life by taking a pottery class during the time I was enrolled in MBA classes. Although I enjoyed pottery, it didn't seem practical to spend an evening getting muddy at a local high school when I should be home studying business books.

I come from a family of artists. My grandmother painted exquisite watercolors, I'm told, although I've never seen her work as she died when I was a toddler. When I was young, my dad would sit at the table on weekend mornings and teach me to draw trees and landscapes. One of my sisters sculpted. As for me, I always loved art, taking classes throughout high school and during the first two years of college.

Somewhere along the line, I realized that I wasn't going to be the next Picasso, and I decided to study something sensible, like business. Back then, I really struggled with mathematics. I nearly flunked pre-calculus my freshman year, and the required calculus class for the business major was the last thing I wanted to take.

I was conflicted. I didn't want to be a starving artist, and I didn't want to be a business major. I compromised by studying advertising and graphic design. It seemed practical, and it wasn't so bad. But somehow, the career choice never felt like me. It made me a shadow of the person I thought I should be.

As I watch the sketchers, most of whom look my age or older, I think that maybe I could start drawing again. The artists congregate together near me, and they pass on their drawings to a gray-haired man with a beret.

"Excusez-moi," I say to him. *"C'est une école pour les arts?"*

He tells me it's not an art school but a two-week art class. He shows me some of their drawings. He invites me to attend a class sometime, and gives me his card. My spirit soars as I imagine myself in Paris immersed in art—spending time studying the masters, developing my artistic eye, enjoying timeless days creating visual inspirations. But realistically, I don't think I'll be back in Paris anytime soon.

After leaving the garden, I don't want to visit any more museums. I'll find a café and relax with a glass of wine watching the people walk by. Along the way, I see an optical shop. I have noticed that the French women wear glasses with square shapes and colorful frames. Maybe new glasses would help me bring a piece of Parisian sophistication home with me.

I walk into the store, and I'm greeted with *"Bonjour"* and some other words I don't understand. I smile. The clerk thinks I'm French!

"Je ne comprends pas," I say. *"Je parle anglais."*

She switches to "Hello, may I help you with something?"

I don't buy glasses, but I'm elated that I have passed for French, at least in the optical shop. The waiter at the café isn't fooled.

"Hello. What would you like?"

I have an idea. Maybe he can help. "I'd like to practice my French. Would you speak to me in French and correct me?"

"Yes, of course."

I order a glass of wine, and the waiter begins my French lesson. He doesn't mind my accent, but he's dismayed at my sentence structure. After I order, I sit facing the street, watching people: men in suits, women dressed in black with impractical shoes, supersized American tourists with cameras draped around their necks.

This lingering afternoon is my last in France. I don't want to go back to the world of "shoulds" and "musts." I long for quiet contemplation, riding my bike, and appreciating the splendor surrounding me.

Maybe it's not too late to make some changes. I can still be an artist—an artist of my own life. I don't have to follow a paint-by-numbers kit. Who said I had to anyway? My life is my canvas, and I can sketch out my vision, fill in the colors, and proudly display my masterpiece for everyone to see. It's up to me to bring the beauty into my world by designing a life filled with vibrancy.

Thank God for France. If I hadn't come here, I may have never taken the time to understand that the hole that I've felt isn't really because of lack of relationship. I've been desperately trying to find a way to feel more complete. One of the most quoted lines from the movie *Jerry McGuire* is, "You complete me." (This is the same phrase that Jim had plagiarized in his card to me.) The truth is that no one can help another feel more whole. Feeling complete comes from feeding our essence and creating a life that radiates joy in our hearts.

I've already started walking on the path of wholeness by following my inner voice instead of my inner critic. It leads me to embrace my passions. Cycling, visiting France, contemplating art—all of these enrich my soul. I need to remember that life isn't about all of the expectations I have for myself or that others have of me. Life feels more complete when I give myself permission to follow my bliss.

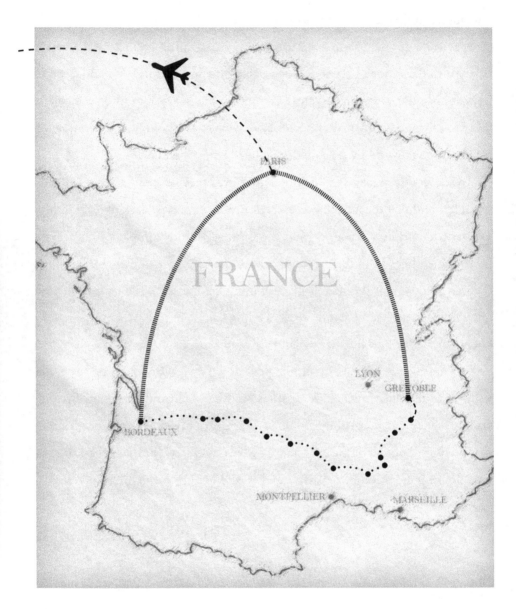

ROUTE NOTES: *Travel by plane from Paris, France, through Salt Lake City and back home to Billings, Montana.*

DISTANCE: *5,547 miles or 8,927 kilometers*

Chapter 25

WELCOME HOME

Alex picked me up at the airport last night, greeting me with a big smile and welcoming hug. At home I saw that everything was in order: the house cleaned, the lawn mowed, and the dogs well fed. All that worry and she did just fine on her own! Oreo, however, never returned and I don't think he'll ever be back. I'm sure he must have had an accident that he didn't survive. I just hope that he left without a lot of pain.

This afternoon I'm back at work. Everyone seems so happy to see me. They tell me they've read my blog and followed my journey across France.

I'm so exhausted from the time change that I know I won't be thinking coherently today. I decide to spend my afternoon tackling mail and email. I start with a large box beside my desk. Looking at the label, I see it's a quarterly shipment from my wine club, which I have sent to work so someone over eighteen can sign for it since I'm not home during the day and Alex is gone most of the year.

In France, it's 9:30 p.m. right now. If I were there, I'd be sipping a glass of red wine in a quaint village rather than sorting mail at my gray metal desk at the bank. I open the box, and I'm surprised by what I see: a bottle of California wine called Pétanque. The label says the name is designed to pay homage to the region of the Rhône Valley in southern France. I smile, remembering the old guys in the dusty town square rolling the metal balls.

It's just a silly marketing ploy, but somehow the bottle of wine seems like a gift from the universe. "Welcome home. Here's a bit of France to remember your travels."

After work, the summertime weekly downtown street party is underway outside my building. I stop and talk with some coworkers from the bank, telling them of my travels in France. I intend to stay for a few minutes and head out for a bike ride on this hot July evening. Someone buys me a glass of wine, and I linger for a while longer.

Everything feels disorienting. Just two days ago I was sitting at a café in Paris, watching men with berets drinking wine. Now I'm back in Montana surrounded by bankers and cowboys drinking beer. Instead of the campground karaoke, I'm listening to worn-out seventies and eighties music sung by a local rock band. There's no struggle to understand the language, no sense of being a foreigner. It feels so easy to fall back into familiar patterns, staying in my comfort zone.

If I were in France, I know I wouldn't just talk to the familiar faces. I'd make an effort to make new friends. I leave the comfort of my bank friends and walk over to one of the cowboys across the street, who is around the same age as the *pétanque* players. I introduce myself; his name is Hank. I ask if I can take his photo.

"Yep," Hank says with his western twang. "No problem."

Through my viewfinder I frame the man dressed in boots, Wranglers, a plaid shirt and a white cowboy hat. His left hand holds his Budweiser; his right rests along his leather belt adorned with a turquoise-studded buckle.

We talk for a while, and he tells me why he moved to Montana decades ago and offers some details about ranch life. He's no different than people halfway around the world: everyone wants to share their story. I realize that I don't need to travel to another country to connect with people. I can extend myself right in my hometown. As much as I'm enjoying my conversation with the cowboy, I'm itchy to jump on my bike since I haven't ridden for five days. I hurry home to change, put my camera in my jersey pocket, and take my favorite scenic route.

As I pedal beside the Yellowstone River on the quiet back roads, I'm renewed by the scenic beauty. I stop to take photos of the fast-moving river and the giant, leafy cottonwood trees rustling in the breeze. Horses, cows, and even llamas and goats graze in the pasture. I don't hear the singing of a mourning dove but the familiar cackle of a pheasant as it scurries across a field.

"J'ai la pêche!" I say out loud as I pedal down the road. I've discovered that having the peach isn't about riding fast, finding true love, or enjoying a traveling adventure. It means taking in the wonder of the world and appreciating the life that I have right here, right now. Tonight, I have the peach.

Fifteen miles down the road, I reach the small town of Laurel where I grew up. It's getting late; I know I should turn around. I continue my journey, passing through town, riding by my old high school, and then climbing cemetery hill. I cycle north of town to the dry plateau with checkerboard wheat fields and sandstone cliffs.

The sun is setting as I reach the summit. I take out my camera to capture its descent. The yellow globe glows vibrantly, but it has mellowed around the edges with halos of burnt orange. The sky has turned a grayish blue, and the clouds are shadows in the big Montana sky. The ball is sliced in half as it meets the horizon and then disappears altogether.

Back on my bike, I begin pedaling in the warm evening. Without lights, I slow down, stay on the shoulder, and take the quickest route to my house. As I ride in the shadows, I realize that the beauty and adventure I sought were always at my doorstep. I only needed to open my eyes to see the treasure that was here all along.

It's good to be home.

The sun sets atop the bluffs north of Laurel, Montana.

SATISFIED
ON MY OWN

Nearly two years after my trip to France, not much has changed outwardly in my life. I still work at the bank, live in the same house, and take my two dogs for walks or runs most every day. My daughter attends the same college, although her days of a college athlete are now behind her.

As for dating, there's still a tendency to jump back into old patterns, particularly in relationships, because that's what I know. I'd like to tell you that when I came back from France, I was through with my relationship with Dante, but it took me more than a year of on-again-off-again interactions before I could finally wean myself away from his charm.

And after France, I have dated but I'm no longer on the relationship merry-go-round. Even though I'd still like a committed relationship, I don't long for one. Day by day, I'm creating a more passion-filled life and evolving into the person my heart calls me to be. And for now, I'm satisfied on my own.

ACKNOWLEDGEMENTS

For more than a decade I've been telling everyone I know: "I want to write a book." The difference between wanting to write and actually writing has happened because of the support of many people.

I appreciate my writing friends who have encouraged me through the years. Thanks to all of the readers of my early drafts. The Night Writers suffered through countless versions of my manuscript. Thanks Jackie Sweiz, Martin Peterson, and Cheryl Moseley for sharing my Fridays to talk about writing and to share some wine. (Thanks also to Mike and Nancy Smith and staff at The Soup Place for hosting us.) There were many readers of my early draft posted on Authonomy.com. Thank you to all who took time to read it and suggest improvements. I'd particularly like to acknowledge Murray Bailey for his extensive review. And to Martin Presse, thanks for helping me finalize the book ending and for stepping in as my speaking coach.

Thanks to my editors and teachers: Kathleen Flinn, Theo Pauline Nestor, TJ Gilles, Christopher Mote, Sue Hart and Tami Haaland. I am also grateful for two local editors who have continued to support my writing: David Crisp from the *Billings Outpost* and Allyn Calton from *Magic City Magazine*.

Special thanks to the friends I met in France. The crew and cyclists on the Wide Open Road Tour were great companions on my journey from Bordeaux to the Alps. I'd like to especially acknowledge Andrew Rowland for being such a compassionate and kind tour leader and Ian Peak for being my no-nonsense friend. The French were especially welcoming: Patrick, Aurora, Benoit, Jessica and Jean, and the *pétanque* players of Saint-Géniez d'Olt. To Matt and Lynn Dassow, I appreciated your hospitality in letting me stay with you in Paris and for being such awesome tour guides.

The cyclists in Billings also deserve recognition. To the Saturday morning group, I know I haven't been out in a while since I've been sitting at home writing my book. But I read your emails and I'm looking forward to the day when I'll have time for cycling. Thanks also to Coach Jay Marschall for teaching me what getting in shape really means. And to his wife, Sarah Keller, thanks for being my riding buddy. It was nice to share the miles with you.

Members of Sunrisers Toastmasters were also very supportive as I did readings instead of speeches during our meetings. Thanks for allowing me to play the part of an author. This helped my confidence in ways I can't explain.

I'd like to acknowledge David Hancock and Rick Frishman from Morgan James Publishing for taking a chance on me. Thanks also to Mitch Mortimer and Daniele Stoddard for their belief in me. Also appreciation is due to Mary Dyre for her help with contract review and to my Web designer, Cynthia Lay.

To all my coworkers at First Interstate Bank, and particularly the Credit Card Division, I have enjoyed the eight years of camaraderie. I particularly want to mention the "marketing sistahs" who make work a lot of fun: Bria Farren, Anjel Kindsfather, Danielle Meyer, Tara Meyers, and Martha Finnick.

To my good friends who have shared my journey, words cannot express my gratitude. You were there when I needed you: Glen Carlson, Diana Larson, Nikki Dolan, Doug Brown, Sandra Schiavon, Frosty and Suzanne Erben, Monica Hildreth, Leslie Blair, Laura Grady, and Alden and Pat Gjevre. Special thanks to

Kathleen Gjevre for caring enough to listen to my dating sagas through the years. My sister, Bonnie Rimert has always been loyal, honest, and loving. I'd also like to acknowledge my parents, Floyd and Norma Rimert, now deceased, who taught me how to be independent in the world. To my Aunt Evelyn and late Uncle Clarence Payette, thanks for being my second parents.

Most of all, I'd like to express my love to my darling daughter, Alex Gjevre. You are a remarkable individual who has taught me so much about pursuing one's dreams. But more than your drive, I am humbled by your big, generous heart. You have showed me how to really love, and I am honored that you are a part of my life. (Special recognition is owed to the MSU Eagles Softball Team and coaches who have been Alex's surrogate family for the past four years.)

And to "Dante," "Jeff," "Jim," and all the other men who have shared my life: thanks for helping me evolve into a better person. I really do love you all and wish each of you the best in life.

$\mathcal{H}$ELPFUL FRENCH EXPRESSIONS

Bonjour		Good day. Used like *hello* during the day.
Bonsoir		Good evening. Used like *hello* during the evening.
Salut		Used as *hi* or as a way to toast before a drink.
Bonne nuit		Good night
Au revoir		Goodbye
Ça-va? *Comment allez-vous?*		How are you? (*Ça-va* is more informal.)
Où-est la toilette?		Where's the toilet? Don't say *bathroom* in French, unless you plan to take a bath.
Je voudrais du vin rouge.		I'd like some red wine.
J'ai la pêche!		Literally means *I have the peach*. You are on top of your game.
Je voudrais votre photo.		I'd like your photo.
Je voudrais un sandwich au jambon et fromage.		I'd like a ham and cheese sandwich. (You can find these everywhere.)

Pardonnez-moi.	Pardon me.
Qu'est-ce que c'est? **?**	What is that?
Je m'appelle ... [insert your name]	My name is ...
Je suis américaine [*américain* for men]	I am American.
C'est mon vélo.	This is my bike.
Allez! Allez! Allez!	Go! Go! Go! – used during bicycle races.

You can learn how to pronounce French words using free online audio dictionaries. A good place to start is *www.online-languages.info*.

$\mathcal{W}$INES ALONG THE WAY: BORDEAUX TO THE ALPS

by Jaclyn Stuart CS, WSET-Certified, Wine Consultant
Co-author of The Complete Idiot's Guide to Wine
& Food Pairing

- **Bordeaux** wine region consists of more than 10,000 wine-producing chateaus. Most of the wines are full-bodied reds that are highly sought after and age-worthy. Permitted grapes include Cabernet Sauvignon, Cabernet Franc, Merlot, Petit Verdot and Malbec. There is more Merlot and Cabernet grown here than anywhere else in the world. White Bordeaux is made from Sauvignon Blanc, Sémillon, and Muscadelle grapes and can range from bone-dry (as in the Entre-deux-Mers sub-region) to sticky sweet (as in the great subregion of Sauternes).

- **Saint-Émilion** is one of the oldest wine appellations of Bordeaux. The area is famous for its rich red wine which is typically blended from red Merlot, Cabernet Franc, and sometimes a bit of Cabernet Sauvignon. They are considered the most robust of Bordeaux wines. The area is named for the village of Saint-Émilion, located in southwest France on the banks of the Dordogne River.

- **Monbazillac** is an area famous for its sweet, honey-tasting wines (with a hint of apricot or peach). The wine blends Sémillon, Sauvignon Blanc, and Muscadelle grapes. The area is located in Monbazillac, France, on the left bank of the Dordogne River.

- **Bergerac** reds and rosés are produced from a blend of at least two of the following grapes: Cabernet Sauvignon, Cabernet Franc, Merlot, and Malbec (known here as Côt), Fer Servadou, or Merille. The reds are similar in taste to Bordeaux wines. Whites are produced from Sémillon, Sauvignon Blanc, Muscadelle, Ondenc, Chenin Blanc, and Ugni Blanc grapes. The whites are dry, crisp, and aromatic with a lingering finish. The area is near Bergerac, France.

- **Côtes de Bergerac**, a wine-growing area around Bergarac, France, is known for reds made from Cabernet Sauvignon, Cabernet Franc, Merlot Noir, and Malbec. They are mellow and soft with a great potential to age. This is basically the same as Bergerac, except that they also produce sweet whites here. The reds are more regulated, and thus thought to be of a higher quality.

- **Pécharmant** wines are produced in the hills to northeast of the Bergarac, France. The red wines are dry, tannic, full-bodied, and fruity. They blend a minimum of three varietals including Cabernet Sauvignon, Cabernet Franc, Malbec, and Merlot.

- **Provence** is France's oldest wine-making region famous for rosé wines, located south of Avignon. The main grape varieties of the region are Syrah, Cinsault, Grenache, Mourvèdre and Tibouren with regulated use of Cabernet Sauvignon and Carignan. The salmon-pink rosés are known to be light and crisp and a great accompaniment to a wide range of cuisines.

- **Côtes du Rhône** is a region which stretches from Vienne in the north to Avignon in the south. The red and rosé wines blend Grenache Noir, Syrah, Cinsault, Carignane, Counoise, and Mourvèdre grapes varieties. The reds are described as full-bodied and robust with balanced tannins and classic herbal scents of the landscape.

- **Châteauneuf-du-Pape** is a wine-growing area located around Châteauneuf-du-Pape and neighboring villages. The name literally translates to "new castle of the Pope" and is named such because Pope John XXII decided to build a summer residence in this area largely because of his adoration for the wine made here. Grenache Noir is the most common variety used for reds, which is blended with up to twelve other varietals to create wines that are known to be rich, earthy, and rustic as they age. Whites may consist of Grenache Blanc, Roussanne, Bourboulenc, Clairette, and Picpoul grapes. The whites taste fruity and flowery, with peach, honeysuckle, and jasmine flavors.

- **Ventoux** red wine comes from the area in the southern Rhône, surrounding the southern side of Mont Ventoux. Grenache, Carignan, Cinsault, Syrah, and Mourvèdre are the most prominently used grapes. The wine is very approachable and fruity, with plum and earthy notes.

ABOUT THE AUTHOR

Nancy Brook is a writer, speaker, business woman, and biker chick. While this is her first book, she has written hundreds of magazine and newspaper articles through the years. In her twenties, she undertook a three-year "writing internship" by starting a newspaper. Possessing a lot of passion but limited business acumen, she packed up her family, moved to Montana, and started a monthly publication with her then husband. The newspaper eventually reached a circulation of 40,000 and Nancy was recognized by the Small Business Administration as Media Advocate of the Year.

Another one of her passions is public speaking. Nancy is an award-winning speaker and fourteen-year member of Toastmasters International. She has won the District Table Topics contest twice and was a regional finalist of the International Speech contest. She has achieved the designation of Advanced Communicator-Gold and currently serves as Area Governor.

Nancy holds an MBA from the University of Montana and has more than twenty-five years experience in marketing. Her favorite activities are jogging, biking, and traveling around the world. She lives in Billings, Montana, with her two hairy herding dogs.